CHOICE POINT

D1348104

NEWHAM LIBRARIES

90800100085723

CHOICE POINT

ALIGN YOUR PURPOSE

HARRY MASSEY &
DAVID R. HAMILTON PhD

HAY HOUSE
Australia • Canada • Hong Kong • India
South Africa • United Kingdom • United States

First published and distributed in the United Kingdom by:
Hay House UK Ltd, 292B Kensal Rd, London W10 5BE.
Tel.: (44) 20 8962 1230; Fax: (44) 20 8962 1239.
www.hayhouse.co.uk

Published and distributed in the United States of America by:
Hay House, Inc., PO Box 5100, Carlsbad, CA 92018-5100.
Tel.: (1) 760 431 7695 or (800) 654 5126; Fax: (1) 760 431 6948 or (800) 650 5115.
www.hayhouse.com

Published and distributed in Australia by:
Hay House Australia Ltd, 18/36 Ralph St, Alexandria NSW 2015.
Tel.: (61) 2 9669 4299; Fax: (61) 2 9669 4144.
www.hayhouse.com.au

Published and distributed in the Republic of South Africa by:
Hay House SA (Pty), Ltd, PO Box 990, Witkoppen 2068.
Tel./Fax: (27) 11 467 8904. www.hayhouse.co.za

Published and distributed in India by:
Hay House Publishers India, Muskaan Complex, Plot No.3, B-2,
Vasant Kunj, New Delhi – 110 070. Tel.: (91) 11 4176 1620; Fax: (91) 11 4176 1630.
www.hayhouse.co.in

Distributed in Canada by:
Raincoast, 9050 Shaughnessy St, Vancouver, BC V6P 6E5.
Tel.: (1) 604 323 7100; Fax: (1) 604 323 2600

Text © Harry Massey and David Hamilton

The moral rights of the authors have been asserted.

All rights reserved. No part of this book may be reproduced by any mechanical, photographic
or electronic process, or in the form of a phonographic recording; nor may it be stored in
a retrieval system, transmitted or otherwise be copied for public or private use, other than
for 'fair use' as brief quotations embodied in articles and reviews, without prior written
permission of the publisher.

The information given in this book should not be treated as a substitute for professional medical
advice; always consult a medical practitioner. Any use of information in this book is at the
reader's discretion and risk. Neither the authors nor the publisher can be held responsible for
any loss, claim or damage arising out of the use, or misuse, or the suggestions made or the
failure to take medical advice.

A catalogue record for this book is available from the British Library.

ISBN: 978-1-84850-552-0

Printed and bound in Great Britain by TJ International, Padstow, Cornwall.

LONDON BOROUGH OF NEWHAM	
90800100085723	
Bertrams	29/05/2012
158.1	£12.99
ANF	NHGS

CONTENTS

CONTENTS

FOREWORD

There is no question that there are a lot of problems in the world today. I am passionate about making a positive difference, and for that reason I am using my entrepreneurial skills to address some of the difficulties we are facing.

When we look at some of the great leaders of the past, such as Gandhi or Nelson Mandela, we see that they represent *positive change*. These individuals stood by a set of principles that have ensured they are remembered today for their compassion, kindness, and forgiveness as much as for the important changes they brought about.

Great change-makers show us that we need to do more than just do certain things. They show us that we need to lead from the inside. We need to *be* the changes.

This is what this book is all about. It is about encouraging people to recognize that the power to change their lives, and the world, is at their fingertips. That power lies in their capacity to change themselves – to become models for the type of world they want to inhabit.

If everyone made just a small change for the better, then great strides could be made in the world, and together we could move more swiftly toward finding solutions to some of the challenges that face us today.

I hope that you will be inspired by this book, and that you will realize how important your own contribution to the world can be. Success unshared is failure.

JOHN PAUL DEJORIA, OCTOBER 2011

PREFACE

In October of 2011, the 7 billionth member of our human family joined us here on Earth. Never in the history of our species have so many people lived together at once, and expected so much from the Earth. At the same time the best minds of our time tell us that now, in the first years of the 21st Century, our expanding global family faces a clear and present danger – the greatest number and magnitude of crises believed to have ever converged on to a single generation in history.

While the record number of people and the crises appear to be related in some ways, they may be linked in others that are unexpected. Maybe it's no accident that only now, when we must solve the greatest threats to our survival, that we also have the greatest number of people that give us more opportunities to do so. Each individual has the power to make choices in his or her life – the very choices that will be the collective answer to the crises of our time. The more choices of peace and balance that we make each day in our lives, for example, the quicker we tip the scales in favor of those choices for our world.

In September of 2005 the journal *Scientific American* released a special edition (vol. 293, no. 3) to inform the world of just how critical our situation really is. The title, 'Crossroads for Planet Earth,' says it all. The emphasis of the edition is that the way we solve the many and simultaneous crises, including our response to climate change, the growing levels of extreme poverty, the emergence of new diseases, the growing shortages of food and fresh drinking water, the growing chasm between extreme wealth and extreme poverty, and the unprecedented demand for energy, will chart the greatest destiny – or seal the darkest fate – of the largest human family to have ever inhabited the Earth. For the first time, the future of our entire species rests upon the choices of a single generation – us – and the choices are being made within a small window of time – now!

Clearly, the key to our success in transcending the crises of our time is based in the way we think of ourselves, the world, and our relationship to choice.

What would it mean to discover that nature creates windows of opportunity that make it easier for us to change the course of our lives at some times more than at others? If we could recognize when such windows appear, we would give ourselves a precious opportunity to 'stack the deck' of success in our favor when it comes to our decisions, both personally and collectively. From intimate relationships that heal our hearts to lifestyle changes that heal our bodies, and even the war and peace that affects us on a global scale, knowing when our choices are more likely to succeed gives us an evolutionary edge to succeed. When it comes to the course of our lives and the future of our world, what could possibly be a more powerful agent of change? While we certainly can make new choices at any time, it makes perfect sense to do so when the cycles and rhythms of nature give them greater potency. The key is to recognize when the greatest moments of choice appear and the cycles that make them possible.

Nature's Choice Points

In a 1957, Princeton University's pioneering physicist Hugh Everett III proposed a scientific theory that describes the power of choice. In a paper titled 'Relative State Formulation of Quantum Mechanics,' he suggested that each time we change an existing course of events we create what can be thought of as a 'fork' in the road of life to accommodate the change. It's this fork of events that becomes the new reality reflecting our choice or, in Everett's view, a new world where the new possibilities unfold. While the equations for Everett's theory appear very complex, what they describe is actually very intuitive. The bottom line is that nature makes room for new outcomes from existing circumstances, and that we have the power to trigger the possibilities.

The key here is that Everett gave a scientific foundation for what we sense in our hearts; when we make a choice in life, our choice shifts the pattern of the past to make room for the new choice and our future. Everett called the moment when such a shift appears a choice point. For our purposes we can think of a choice point as a bridge that connects us in the present with new outcomes and possibilities that become our future. Knowing that choice points exist, however, is only half of the story. Knowing when a choice point occurs is the rest of the key to using them. This is where the power of cycles comes in.

Beginnings, Endings, and Beginnings

We live in a universe of cycles. Some cycles are brief and obvious, like the changing from night to day or the cycles of the moon and the seasons. Some cover vast periods of time and are not so obvious. The 5,125-year-long cycle of a Great World Age, such as the one that began on August 11, 3114 BC and ends on December 21, 2012, is a perfect example. No one living today was alive when the cycle began. We depend upon the written records and the indigenous traditions of the past to tell us about such cycles.

The knowledge of a how a cycle begins and ends is the key to using choice points. Whether the cycle lasts for one day or thousands of years, the principle of when it starts, when it ends, and what happens in between is the same. Each cycle begins with a seed event – something that sets a pattern of energy in to motion. Before the pattern repeats itself as the next cycle, however, it ends with a window of time where the pattern is absent. This place of no patterns is the choice point of the cycle.[1] The choice point is the greatest window of opportunity for each cycle because it holds the greatest opportunity to change patterns of the past before they repeat. In this way, cycles of time and our power of choice are closely related.

Our ancestors understood choice points. They knew, for example, that the twilight at the end of the day is when our prayers are most potent. It's at this time that they called the 'crack between the worlds,' when it's not quite daylight and not quite nighttime, that we have the opportunity to set a new pattern in to motion for the day that follows. In a similar way, our most ancient and cherished traditions remind us that we are living the rarest of twilights on a global level – the crack between the end of the Fifth World Age and the beginning of the Sixth. And just as dawn and dusk become the choice point that divides the night and the day, our twilight between the years 1980 and 2016 is the choice point that divides our World Ages. This 36-year-long choice point is our opportunity to reset the patterns of war, suffering, and destruction from the past, before the next cycle begins. And it's a good thing that we have such an opportunity. The elders of the past and scientists of today both tell us that our future looks dim unless we embrace our time of change and rethink the thinking and unsustainable ways of life that we've created for the last 5,000 years. Sir Martin Rees, Professor of Astrophysics at the University of Cambridge, suggests that we have only a *'50:50 chance of surviving the 21st century without a major setback.'* The good news is that our power of choice gives new meaning, and new hope, for a bright future.

The Hope

The best science of our time, when it's married to the wisdom of our past, confirms that we still have the ways and means to shift our time of crises into a time of life-affirming emergence – a golden age of hope and possibility. We can create a new world based upon actionable and sustainable principles rooted in the core understanding of our deepest truths. The key is simply this: the better we know ourselves, the clearer the choices in our lives become.

My sense is that the crises of our time and our destiny are intimately entwined. The fact that so many pieces of our lives are being redefined at once, and so many changes are converging during one small window of time, seemingly overnight, appears to be more than just a coincidence. We can think of this convergence as a cosmic reality check. Within the space of just a few short years, we get to see which choices we've made as a civilization work and which ones don't; we can review which systems are sustainable and which ones aren't. And in full view of the broken and failed systems, we must choose: Do we work to embrace new ways of living that give us what we need in clean, sustainable ways that honor us and our world? Or do we fight among ourselves to prop up old and unsustainable ways of living that will eventually break again and leave us hanging in the abyss of the same choices again at a later time?

If we can consider how the choices we make each day fit into the bigger picture, then their role becomes clear. Our individual choices are the collective foundation for our families, communities, nations and the future of the world. With these principles in mind, clearly our ability to choose wisely is paramount to our lives.

It's for these very reasons that the wisdom in *Choice Point* is so much more than simply a collection of information – it's a template for change. It holds the tools to make the change, as well as the key that unlocks the secrets to successful choices in your life. Woven throughout this book is the collective wisdom from some of the worlds leading thinkers, scientists, visionaries, and luminaries sharing how they've made pivotal choices for themselves that led to the fruition of their life passions. And it's precisely because everyone learns differently that this book holds such powerful tools. In the chapters that follow you have the opportunity to test your beliefs and passions, identify your skills, and reveal the spark of your own life purpose. As you do so, you will cultivate the wisdom to recognize the true power of your choices, the courage to choose for yourself, and the strength to follow through on your choices.

Choice Point is the only book of its kind. It was designed for you, as your personal blueprint of transformation. I invite you to explore this book yourself to see where it leads you. In doing so, you align yourself with a global community that is answering the evolutionary impulse that draws us to become better people, choose better lives, and make the world a better place!

GREGG BRADEN, NOVEMBER 2011

INTRODUCTION

We believe we are facing a Choice Point in our history and that in order to transform the world for the better, we need to transform ourselves. In the course of making this book, we traveled around the world to meet and interview some of the most significant change agents on our planet. We wanted to learn how they were able to transform themselves, not only to master their own lives, but also to make a positive difference in the world.

Throughout our conversations, a simple three-step formula presented itself again and again: one that can be used to create real and lasting change in the world.

1) Understand Your World

2) Align Your Purpose

3) Be the Change

Understand Your World means to understand the nature of how and why things happen. This book explores fractal (repeating) patterns and cycles in nature and in the cosmos, from the very small right up to the very large. We explore how, despite the idea that we can exercise free will, we are not separate from these patterns that affect our lives.

We will show you that the more you understand the patterns and cycles that surround you, the greater the ability you will have to fully master life and exercise your free will to create the life that you want. Understand Your World helps you to predict future possibilities, so you can distinguish between patterns that are likely and those that are unlikely.

In Align Your Purpose we show you how to make choices to align yourself with patterns and cycles, just as if you'd steered a canoe into a current on a river. When you align yourself with a pattern, you flow with it. And as you do so, you take in the fruits of the current, almost as if you are allowing destiny to unfold.

We also explore the idea that the universe can be described as 'information,' and that we are constantly exchanging information with it. Therefore we align with patterns when we exchange information with them. But as fractal patterns are scalar, that is they scale up in ever-increasing sizes, if we are exchanging information with them, we scale up with them.

Aligning Your Purpose also shows you how, if you truly align your purpose with the cycles and harmonious patterns of the world, then what you do can scale up to a level beyond your wildest dreams. This part of the book also discusses the types of patterns that are most harmonious in the world, namely those that are supported by nature or by large numbers of people. In the current climate, many harmonious patterns are actually those that serve others in some way; those that help others to grow and expand, and experience a healthier, happier, and more fulfilling life.

The third part of the book, Be the Change, explores our theory that if we change ourselves we can change the world. This is built around a principle that we call 'matching.' Matching is simple to understand: the more similar things are, the more information and energy they will exchange with each other. When we apply that to succeeding in life and making a positive difference in the world, the key is how to be the best match within ourselves for the patterns that we wish to align ourselves with. To do this we need to look within ourselves, and to change ourselves to be that match. And, crucially, if we match with a pattern that benefits others, we scale up with that pattern. And the pattern affects others along the way. They align with it too, as it grows. And thus when we choose to be the change in life, we can change the world.

Be the Change also encourages you to align your life's purpose with patterns that will support the creation of a better world and therefore, as you *become* the changes you will need to be, you will help to change the world.

Behind Choice Point

The idea to create Choice Point began a number of years ago. In my opinion, I had screwed my life up, big time. For seven years, my life seemed to be over because I spent a significant portion of it staring up at the ceiling, not being able to move for more than a few hours each day. I had severe chronic fatigue syndrome, and I believe this was entirely self-inflicted. I had been on a self-destructive, hedonistic streak that arose out of negative self-beliefs about my sexuality.

The questions I ask myself now, though, as I look back at that time in my life are: 'Did I purposefully choose those years in bed?' No. 'Did I create it?' Well, yes. 'Or was it even part of my destiny?'

Looking back at how that crisis defined my purpose has actually led me to create a successful business and produce a successful documentary film – *The Living Matrix* – so destiny does seem to have played its card. Free will or destiny? I always wondered about that. Would I be where I am today without that crisis? I'm pretty sure I wouldn't.

I had a very significant turning point in my journey from disease and misery to being able to build a successful business and a life of abundance. I simply decided that the way to get myself better was to try to understand what was *really* behind health – how the body really worked – and I determined to create a wellness system that would enable people to be able to work out what was wrong with them from home and, more importantly, give them a way of getting themselves better again.

I figured that if I could do that, I would get better along the way. I had no idea how this could be done, or who would help me, but because I had literally nothing to lose – I had no life really to speak of after all – I thought I might as well try.

That journey was an extremely tough one, compounded by the fact that I had very limited time each day for thinking; and that thinking was extremely foggy, as fellow sufferers from chronic fatigue will understand. Against all the odds, really – I had no business experience, not even any work experience; I had heavily compromised health; and I'd even pretty much forgotten my social skills, having been holed up for seven years – I succeeded. Incredible coincidences happened for me, and NES Health (the company I created) started to grow and my own health greatly improved.

What, though, was really at the center of this success? What allowed destiny to work for me? It was something incredibly simple.

At that Choice Point in my life, I decided to align with a purpose that was bigger than my selfish desire to get myself healthy, putting myself as a servant to make others better. Simply aligning with a purpose that was harmonious to others enabled patterns that are inherent in nature to support me. And, in turn, I got healthy too.

Could I have done that earlier and avoided those years of suffering? Unlikely. Without the intense misery that I experienced, I wouldn't have had the drive to learn, and to do what I needed to do. Could I have made that change later? Again unlikely, as it was at that time that I had the opportunity to radically change my life and move to America, where I discovered the information I needed to put my vision into action. If I hadn't gone there, I'm fairly certain my health would have carried on deteriorating beyond the point of being able to do anything at all.

It seemed to me that life has patterns that unfold and that some points in our life are more significant than others – where the choices we make can have a much more significant effect on our life than others.

This book is about those Choice Points, those windows of opportunity where you have the choice to do something different, so that you are supported rather than fighting against the patterns unfolding in nature. It's about how, in those moments, you can recognize those patterns and align your purpose with them, so that they will help you in your life and make a difference in the world.

This book shares practical examples from some of the most significant leaders and thinkers of our day, showing how much of their success pivots on them thoroughly researching and understanding their world so they are able to align their purpose and actions with what will succeed. They understand that through recognizing and aligning with key patterns, the incredible becomes possible.

This book, and our Align Your Purpose Transformation Program (see p.217), also show you how free will and destiny intertwine, and how you can take the advantages of both through aligning your purpose.

They will help you find your purpose, turn that into success in your life, and make a difference to the world. They will tell you precisely how real masters of life are succeeding, and explain how you can recognize and take advantage of the Choice Points and patterns occurring in your own life so you can jump to a better cycle, one that is better for you and better for the world.

The book begins by taking a look at the current state of the world and asking the question: 'Do we want to create a better world?'

HARRY MASSEY, SEPTEMBER 2011

OPENING

'We're in a crisis of birth toward a more positive future and each one of us is part of it.'

BARBARA MARX HUBBARD

Choice Point is a term borrowed from physics. It is a place of branching or forking. It is a point of possibility. We can also think of it as a fork in a road that creates another road. The idea behind Choice Point is that we can choose which of those two roads to travel down. If we make the same choices that we have made in the past, then we will choose the road that will lead us to the same problems, only on a larger scale.

But we can also choose the *other* road, the one that can lead us into a better world – a world of peace, of fairness, of education, of harmony.

We live in a world of cycles. Our hearts beat cyclically, we breathe cyclically, even our DNA spiral is a cycle. We sleep, then wake, then sleep again: a natural process driven by the biochemistry of our bodies, which itself is driven by the cyclic rotation of the Earth, exposing us to cyclic pulses of the Sun's rays. Our social lives run in cycles too, and we believe, even though it is not entirely obvious, that many world events are also cyclic.

A Choice Point emerges when one cycle ends and a new one is about to begin. It is a window of time in which our choices can have a potent, lasting effect on our lives. We believe that the number and severity of the crises now facing us indicate that a cycle is coming to an end and that a Choice Point exists on a global scale. American social entrepreneur Bill Drayton says, *'I believe that right now we are at the biggest Choice Point in our history.'* The question is, will we make the same choices that led to these crises?

Writer and futurist Barbara Marx Hubbard says: *'I think what is unique about this time on planet Earth is that we've hit a global set of crises: pollution, overpopulation, climate change, global warming. All of these together could lead to a collapse of our civilization.'* She believes that we cannot continue in this way because it is unsustainable.

Twelve-year-old Birke Baehr, a youth advocate for environmentally friendly agriculture, is also concerned about the sustainability of the road we are currently on. *'One thing I've figured out through my research,'* he says, *'is that a lot of big companies and conglomerates are messing with the environment, and we don't need that happening.'* Wise beyond his years, Birke realizes that there are a lot of problems facing humanity today. *'I don't want to be inheriting some big pile of poo at the age of 30 or 40!'* he says. *'That's just not right to me. I think we need to take better care of our Earth and have it in pristine shape for generations 20 or 30 years down the road.'*

We believe that if we continue on the road we are on, we will inevitably run into more trouble. As Einstein famously said: *'We cannot solve problems by using the same kind of thinking we used when we created them.'*

So do we want to continue on the same road? Former politician and antiwar campaigner Tony Benn shares a powerful personal experience that illustrates the magnitude of what we are capable of when we *don't* make the right choices.

'At the end of the war I was in the Royal Navy and I heard about the Hiroshima bomb on the radio,' Tony recalls. *'Later, I went to Hiroshima and it made a huge impression on me. I was taken round by a guide and on the pavement was a little mark. I asked the guide why he was showing me that. "Because that's where a child was sitting when the bomb dropped; the heat was so great that the child was vaporized," he replied.*

'The heat was such the child melted, and then became dust and blew away. All that was left of it was the mark. And next to the mark was a twisted bit of metal and the guide said, "That was the child's lunch box." And of course, the heat couldn't vaporize the metal, but it contorted it into a hideous shape. So there was the mark and the bit of twisted metal. It was all that was left of a human being.'

But we *can* make better choices than those we've made in the past. Barbara Marx Hubbard gives us hope when she says, '*We have a crisis and we have the opportunity for the next stage of evolution. There is an emergence of a desire for positive use of power and positive use of technology, like in energy. Or positive development of health technology, or positive development of food production that is sustainable and able to support humanity.*'

But will we act? Tony Benn captures our sentiments when he says, '*I think there are two flames burning in every human heart in every period in history: the flame of anger against injustice, and the flame of hope that you can build a better world.*'

He believes we can solve our problems and change the world for the better. '*I have huge confidence in young people,*' he says. '*They are the first generation in human history to have the capacity to destroy the human race, and they have to decide how they are going to deal with the problems. And I think if they are addressed properly, they become a very powerful force for change.*'

Adoptive and foster parent Jodi Orton says: '*I'm very hopeful that this generation is seeing what greed and power have done. I'm hopeful they are learning to work as a team, and that they're learning to reach out and make changes. But I'm also hopeful that with this, a level of kindness will come about, and that we'll learn once again to care about the masses and be far less individualized.*'

When we look around us we can see there are pockets of change everywhere. Later in the book you will read about some of the inspiring philanthropic work undertaken by some of the change agents we spoke to, including entrepreneurial businessmen James Caan, John Paul DeJoria, Bill Drayton, and Sir Richard Branson. You will also read about amazing personal transformations, including that of Brett Moran – a former crack addict who became an addiction-recovery specialist.

Change *is* possible, and it starts with each of us in our own hearts and minds. The big change we have to make is a shift from our love of power – which we believe has produced many of the problems that we face today – to embracing the power of love.

When we embrace the power of love, and that power infuses our lives, our actions change, and we become much more sustainable and much more supportive of others in their hopes and dreams. The power of love can help us to find solutions to our problems and help us to build a better world *together*.

Bill Drayton believes that the power of love has its roots in empathy. Reflecting on the starvation and malnutrition we often see in developing countries, he says, '*If we lived in a world where people's lives were driven by love and the skill of empathy, I don't think this would be happening. We have mechanisms that say those people are different from us, and then we don't feel responsible. We've got to tear down those barriers; we've got to recognize that all life deserves respect, that we are not separate.'*

With this simple change inside, we can begin to change the world.

In the first part of this book, Understand Your World, you will begin your journey of change. You will learn about the cycles and patterns in the world, how they influence your experiences in life, and how you can use them to make better choices.

PART 1
UNDERSTAND YOUR WORLD

CHAPTER 1
THE COMMON THREAD

'Fractals open up a completely new way of thinking about reality and the rules behind it.'

PROFESSOR IAN STEWART

If we want to make the right choices when we are faced with crises, it helps if we understand our world, how and why things happen, and *why* we face crises in the first place. As we come to grasp all this, we can see crises for what they really are: opportunities not only to survive, but to grow and to prosper.

In this part of the book we explore the cycles and patterns that occur in nature and in the cosmos. We also look at how, because our lives are embedded within these cycles and patterns, they also follow cycles and patterns.

We all experience ups and downs, gains and losses, easy times and harder ones, and many aspects of our lives repeat themselves. But if we want to change our lives, and the world, for the better, it is important to understand why these patterns seem to be the way of our lives, and learn to work *with them* rather than *against them.*

This takes us into the world of fractals – patterns that are similar on all scales that you look at them. For instance, a repeating pattern in a person's life – where the same kind of thing happens at different times, perhaps interspersed by weeks, months, or even years – is a fractal pattern. There is a pattern running through his or her life story. A repeating pattern in the world is also a fractal pattern.

We will now explain why such patterns occur, so that you can understand your world better and even look ahead and predict what might be around the corner.

Fractals in Nature and in the Cosmos

'If you zoom in on a fractal, magnify it, look more closely at it, you will see either something that looks very similar, or almost the identical shape on a smaller scale.'
PROFESSOR IAN STEWART

A fractal is a shape that can be split up into parts so that each of the parts resembles the shape of the whole. The principle is called 'self-similarity,' because each smaller part is similar (though not always identical) to the whole.

The mathematician Benoît Mandelbrot coined the term 'fractal' in 1975, deriving it from the Latin term 'fractus,' which means 'broken.' When you zoom in on any part of a fractal, you'll see a replica of the whole thing. Zoom in even farther, and you'll see another replica, and so on. The pattern repeats itself at different scales of magnification.

Fern Leaves and Snowflakes

Fractal patterns are all around us. Take the leaf of a fern – if you look closely at any one part of the leaf, you will see it resembles the whole leaf in its overall shape and texture. Snowflakes are also fractal. If you focus on any one part of one you will see something that is similar to the whole snowflake, again with approximately the same shape and texture. In both these examples, you'll notice that the whole leaf or snowflake is an approximate, scaled-up replica of a tiny fern or snowflake.

These are two of the many fractals we can observe in nature, but what about out in the cosmos? Are there really big fractals too?

Ian Stewart, Emeritus Professor of Mathematics at Warwick University in the UK believes that the whole universe is fractal. *'Astronomers have discovered that the solar system is planets clumped around a star, and then there is big gap to the next star system,'* he explains. *'But then the stars clump together in galaxies. The galaxies clump together in galactic clusters. The galactic clusters clump together into galactic superclusters, and then there are huge voids without any matter at all. The universe is not uniform. It is not smooth. It is lumpy on all scales.'*

So the fractal pattern in the cosmos is of interconnected structures in 'clumps' and then large areas of little or no matter that are the same on ever-increasing scales. The same texture (of 'clumps' and 'gaps') repeats itself at different levels throughout the universe.

But interestingly, it's not just in the cosmos and in nature that we see this type of pattern. At a specific resolution, an image of the human brain's neural net could be mistaken for a galactic image. Even though they are vastly different in size, our brains and the cosmos have the same 'texture.' We also see the same kind of texture in society. Just as galaxies cluster together in the galactic network, and brain cells cluster together in the neural network, humans cluster together in social networks and in towns and cities. So the same pattern seems to exist on all these scales. Could there be a connection, a thread that runs through all this on all scales?

The laws of physics govern all structures in the universe – including neural and cosmic networks – and they originate at the subatomic level. So it is unsurprising then, that when we zoom into things on smaller scales we also find fractal patterns.

Quantum Fractals

'We have fractals from the largest scale in the universe right the way down to the internal structure of fundamental particles.' PROFESSOR IAN STEWART

We can see fractal patterns on a very small scale in a phenomenon known as Brownian motion, which was first described by botanist Robert Brown in 1827 after he observed the seemingly random, zig-zag movements of tiny grains of pollen on the surface of water.

If we drew the paths taken by grains of pollen exhibiting Brownian motion, we would see that they 'dance' around the same areas for a while, creating apparent clusters, before moving to a different area and dancing around that. And if we placed that drawing alongside an image of a human's neural network, a social network, or a galactic network, we'd see a striking similarity in the texture of all three. They have the same pattern, and that pattern is fractal.

Brownian motion came to public attention in 1905, when Einstein explained why the pollen grains moved in the way that they did. He showed that it was because tiny molecules of water were crashing against the sides of the grains. (Imagine the pollen grains as tiny beach balls in a swimming pool being nudged left and right as people fire at them with peashooters.) So the fractal pattern of the movements of the pollen grains was actually caused by the behavior of much smaller molecules.

Scaling down from molecules to the quantum level, subatomic particles are known to change their state (their direction and energy) in an erratic way. And this behavior is also seemingly random – just like Brownian motion. So we get the same pattern in the cosmos, in society, in the brain, with grains of pollen, in movements of molecules, and even in subatomic particles. It is a fractal pattern.

While we can't say for certain that there is an actual relationship between the behavior and structure of the very small and that of the gigantic, it seems likely, as Ian Stewart explains: *'If there is the possibility of fractal behaviour down on very small scales, it is quite reasonable to suppose it might translate in some way to similar kinds of structure for larger objects,'* he says. *'So I think it is actually reasonable to suggest that the fractal structure is unifying the whole of nature and it is to do with the way that the laws of nature produce structure in the universe.'*

And since we are a part of nature and therefore affected by its patterns, we can start to see how aspects of our world, and our own lives, form patterns that may be a simple consequence of these natural patterns.

Let's take a look at some of the natural patterns that affect us.

Cycles, Cycles Everywhere

'Most universally ancient texts and traditions, and the wisdom of our past, tell us that we live in a universe of cycles, and cycles within cycles, nested in cycles.' GREGG BRADEN

Another fractal pattern that exists from the quantum level right through the cosmos is the pattern of cycles, or oscillations. Subatomic particles oscillate, or vibrate. They can be thought of as waves and their in-out, up-down, on-off, back-forth behavior is cyclic. And we can see cycles everywhere, from the very small to the very, very large.

As Ian Stewart points out, it is reasonable to assume that there is a connection between behavior at the quantum level and in the larger patterns in the universe. The universe as we know it possibly began as a quantum phenomenon, before scaling up from the Big Bang to its current size, so we might even consider that the cycles we see in the universe are actually scaled-up versions of quantum behavior. They don't just share a common structure, they might in fact be much more connected than that, with larger behavior in some way a consequence of smaller behavior.

US author and teacher Gregg Braden believes that the cycles throughout the universe do indeed begin at the subatomic level. *'One of the questions that comes up frequently in scientific and philosophical conversations about the nature of our reality is this: now that we know we live in a fractal universe, where do the fractals begin?'* he says. *'What is the primary trigger that begins a fractal? It appears that the seed, the beginning of a fractal, is simply an oscillation of energy. It is an energy form that puts into motion a series of oscillations and patterns that ripple through the fabric of the stuff that our world is made of.'*

Gregg suggests that the basic oscillations of the quantum world somehow 'scale up' so that we see oscillations, or cycles, everywhere in nature, at every scale. In biology, for instance, the double helix structure of DNA is actually like a wave in 3-D, carving out a circle that goes upward in a spiral, or cycle.

German author and medical doctor Rainer Viehweger highlights some other oscillations found in biology. *'In the heartbeat, the rhythms are oscillations,'* he explains. *'Breathing is an oscillation. All things done rhythmically are oscillations.'* He believes we should consider everything that moves to be an oscillation, or part of one, and gives a less obvious example, something that is still a cycle, though, and a consequence of genetics: *'When you go for a walk you oscillate,'* he points out, *'because your legs move with a frequency.'*

Cosmic Cycles and Biological Cycles

The phenomenon of cycles is something that we see in biology then, but it is also something that we see on a cosmic scale. The Moon revolves around the Earth, the Earth spins and it revolves around the Sun, and the Sun revolves around the galaxy. The Earth also tilts and wobbles, producing cycles of climatic variations, as well as what are know as 'precession of the equinoxes' – great cosmic cycles of approximately 26,000 years.

And because we live amid these cosmic cycles, they affect us too. The spinning of the Earth – a cycle of 24 hours – creates the cycle of night and day, which in turn produces cyclic variations in our bodies. Hormones, including melatonin, respond to UV light and regulate our sleep patterns. So the cycle of night and day produces natural movements in the levels of these hormones.

The Earth's cycle around the Sun also gives us the four seasons, which produce cyclic variations in the concentrations of UV light that we are exposed to, affecting everything from skin pigmentation and vitamin D levels to our mental and emotional wellbeing and propensity to some illnesses.

The cycle of the Moon affects us too. It has been shown to tie in with women's menstrual cycles, which are roughly of the same duration. One study of 305 women found that approximately one third had lunar period cycles (an average cycle length of 29.5 days). The study concluded that there was a 'lunar influence on ovulation.' Another study found that a statistically significant number of women started menstruation around the time of a new Moon.[1,2]

Cycles in Nature

Nature, too, reacts to these cosmic cycles and goes through cycles of its own. Trees grow leaves and shed them again, in sync with the cycle of the seasons. Plants grow and die, and animals hibernate and wake. And thus we experience cyclic variations in the food that is available for us to eat, which gives us cyclic variations in the nutrients in our diets.

In evolution by natural selection, the cycles and fractal patterns of nature would have acted like a current that steered aspects of evolution in a particular way. Evolution is about adapting to the environment, but the environment is regulated by cycles in nature, so the human genome evolved amid cycles in nature and was, to an extent, steered by it.

This probably explains why we are so affected by natural cycles today. It is not possible to extract ourselves from the effects of nature. Nature happens, and we're part of it.

Our lives, then, are affected by the cycles in the cosmos and in nature. Some cycles are short, such as night and day, and their effects are obvious. Others are so long that they take many generations to pass, like the Hallstatt Cycle, a cycle of approximately 2,300 years that has been linked with climatic variations. But, in the same way that the onset of day is short and fast relative to the entire period of night, as each cycle comes to a close, the changes as a new cycle passes become more rapid. (This is something that we explore later in the book.)

The existence of natural cycles suggests that there is a degree of order hidden behind what sometimes seem to be random and chaotic world events. In fact, we can think of these cycles as pulling us through time in certain directions.

Cycles in Time

'Some of the cycles occur on scales of time that are so huge, thousands of years, that no one living at the beginning of the cycle is living when the cycle completes. However, we still live the conditions of those cycles.' GREGG BRADEN

As Einstein discovered, space and time are intimately connected. So, just as we find fractal patterns in space – in fern leaves and snowflakes – we also find them in time. We don't usually think of fractals in this way, but it is a useful thing to do to help us understand how cycles affect our lives.

The cosmic cycles that produce cycles in nature are also cycles in time. So just as snowflakes and fern leaves are patterns in space, so cosmic cycles are patterns in time. The Earth's cycle around the Sun is a pattern in time of 365 days, and the cycle of night and day, which spans 24 hours, is also a pattern in time. Each time a cycle comes around, we get certain effects in nature and in our lives.

Some cycles in time are less obvious and span longer periods, but just as night and day can force physiological, emotional (due to hormone changes), and even behavioral changes on us, so these longer cycles may also force, or at least nudge, changes on us.

Climate Cycles

We know, for instance, that in addition to our unsustainable behaviors, part of the climate-change phenomenon is related to the activity of the Sun, which suggests that part of climate change is actually part of a great cycle in time. The effects of this cycle include changes in the Earth's biodiversity as temperatures on its land surfaces and in its oceans rise and fall, and behavioral changes in us as we scramble to preserve particular resources.

The El-Niño weather phenomenon is also a cycle in time. A 56-year study of the relationship between weather patterns and conflicts, published in the world's leading scientific journal, *Nature,* in 2011, found that in countries where El-Niño exerts its effects there is an increased risk of civil war at those times.[3] So, as cycles in time can affect our behavior, it doesn't take too great a stretch of the imagination to consider that other, apparently human-created events, might also be related to cycles in time.

In 2003, the Federal Reserve Bank of Atlanta found a correlation between the activity of the Sun, which is cyclic, and the behavior of the world's stock markets.[4] We cannot rule out the possibility therefore that the economic crisis that began in 2008 is somehow related to the Great Depression of 1929. It could be part of a great cycle in time that influences us, just like the wind blows a flower. The cycle is largely invisible to us. It is not as clear as night and day, but it is around us.

So, as cycles exist at all scales of reality, as well as in human biology, we should seriously consider that any two or more similar events that repeat themselves might be part of a cycle. There may not be a connection at all, but we cannot dismiss the idea on first hearing, just because it doesn't seem likely to us.

Our Choice Point

It's not these physical events themselves that are the cycle, though. It's the conditions that exist as part of the cycle that make such events more likely. El-Niño itself doesn't force war, but it creates certain conditions, such as poor harvests and hotter temperatures, that increase the likelihood of it happening. Similarly, the cycle of the seasons doesn't force automatic behavior, where we are guided like automatons to put on cooler or warmer clothes. Rather, the winter cycle, for instance, creates the conditions of cold so that we then make a decision to dress appropriately.

And, of course, if these economic and natural events are connected to a cycle, it does not necessarily mean that they will happen again, that each time such a cycle ends there will be another disaster. The cycle influences the *conditions*, but we don't have to make the same choices that we did on the previous cycle. It only means that there is a seeming vulnerability as a cycle like this ends and a new one begins.

This vulnerability represents a small window of time in the cycle in which our choices have the greatest impact. As Gregg Braden says, '*Each time the cycle comes to an end, it opens a window of opportunity called a Choice Point.*' It is our *response* to the conditions brought about by cycles that determines the outcomes in our world. Our choices at a Choice Point determine the future.

But how do we know when we are facing a Choice Point? We believe that we are facing one right now as we struggle to make decisions that will restore the economic stability of the world, as we search for peaceful solutions to conflict, as we look for solutions to climate change. Our choices at this time will greatly affect our future. As we emphasize throughout this book, when we make the highest choices, those that are in harmony with the needs of humanity, we end the cycle in a different way from before and start a new cycle in a much better way. Our actions, however small, can change everything.

So, we've learned how fractal patterns and cycles in nature and the cosmos affect us. We will now consider that, as we are actually a part of nature and have evolved within nature's cycles, it is reasonable to believe that aspects of our own lives exhibit fractal, cyclic behavior, too.

Personal Patterns

'There are certain events where, in a sense, it is almost as if a kind of pressure is building up for something to happen. And when it reaches a critical level, it will happen.' PROFESSOR IAN STEWART

Most people are aware of the repeating patterns in their lives. The way in which the same issue or problem crops up over and over again, at least until it is resolved. Let's consider the possibility that these events are in some way connected.

Ian Stewart believes that on a global scale, certain events – including natural disasters and shifts in politics – occur when pressure builds up in the system. *'With political swings from one party to another, or from a particular political point of view to another, you get these big swings roughly in cycles, but with lots of little fluctuations in between. It's irregular, but it has a definite sort of texture to it,'* he explains.

And he says we can relate these kinds of events to the texture of our own lives, too. '*Individual lives are like that: you get the big triumphs; you get the great disasters,*' he points out. '*But it is not that you start with a big triumph and then, very, very steadily you decline until it is turned into a huge disaster. There will be mini triumphs and mini disasters along the way, and the whole texture of your life will be ups and downs from one minute to the next as well as from one year to the next.*'

So the texture of life events are cyclic, not as regular as the ticking of a clock, but definitely cyclic.

It Happens Again and Again

Our lives are not a blank canvas on which only our thoughts and actions shape what happens to us. In fact, cycles exert a considerable influence on the conditions that we meet in life. Our personal power lies in the choices that we make within the conditions that unfold around us.

Let's look at some of the typical cycles in our lives. As a rule, most people go through cycles of financial abundance and scarcity. Some meet the same kinds of people as they go through their lives; others may even marry the 'same' person three times, so to speak – they have different partners but are beset by the same kinds of problems in each relationship.

Gregg Braden observes that some events in our lives will repeat themselves until we do something different, until we make different choices. '*The fractal pattern of my life, if I choose to do nothing, will probably continue and perpetuate the same patterns of success or failure, and relationships or career,'* he says.

'Again and again it will show up in my personal life. It will show up in my family. It will show up in my friendships. It will show up in my career. Again and again, in precisely the same kinds of patterns, unless I choose to make a change, a little change in the way I think about myself, or the way I choose to respond to the crises or challenges of my life.'

As Gregg suggests, the key to breaking the repetitive events of a cycle is to make different *choices* from those we have made in the past. If we do this – perhaps by making a change within ourselves – we will experience a different future from before. It's as if the pattern breaks down, or the cycle touches us in a different way. *'Those little patterns, those little changes for me are the shifts and the fractals that allow me to launch a new trajectory of a different destiny,'* Gregg says.

So, we can change the outcome of cycles in our personal lives by making inner changes. Then, as the next cycle comes around, our new state of being meets it in a new way and so we experience a different set of circumstances in our lives; we meet the circumstances that reflect our new selves.

Breaking Out

Let's imagine that you decide to make a change in yourself. Instead of sitting in your chair every day, uninterested in going outside, you decide that from now on, you are going to live your life to the full. So when the next cycle comes around – the following morning – you get up and go out to meet life. The change within you is met by a new cycle of nature (daybreak) and all that comes with it.

Rather than the cycles just returning to the same place, then, our lives can spiral upward (and sometimes downward). A spiral is what we get when a cycle moves through time. Jack Canfield, coauthor of the *Chicken Soup for the Soul* series of books, describes it as *'... spiraling up. We often return to places and say, "wait, I was here before." But we are not down there again, we're up a level. And so we and our lives spiral up, toward a higher consciousness, even though we revisit old patterns of behavior or often dysfunctional patterns.'*

This sort of thing, where our lives move in a positive direction through cycles, happens all the time, but invisibly. We are part of, and in sync with, lots of patterns and cycles. Each change we make within ourselves – let's say for now these are positive, healthy changes – means that when the next cycle comes along, our lives unfold in a different way. This is what personal growth is all about. It is about becoming the next, better version of ourselves so that we meet new cycles in new and improved ways.

When we don't make any changes within ourselves, though, we repeat the same cycles over and over again. And when social, economic, and cultural events repeat themselves, our firmly held mindsets are exposed to and fertilized by these events in repetitive patterns. We might complain that some of these events are negative to us, but just recognizing that we are experiencing a cycle opens up an opportunity to change, or make a different decision – to choose another way. And when we make that change, the next time the cycle comes along, things are different, because *we* are different.

So, an understanding of the patterns and cycles in our world brings great opportunities, as Gregg Braden explains: '*I thought if we could understand the nature of cycles in our lives, it would help to give meaning to what appear to many to be meaningless events that are happening in our world today – the chaos of war, of economic collapse, and environmental disasters.*' And it also makes us aware that we have a *choice*, because we can see we may have encountered the same kinds of circumstances in the past because we were making the same choices, but without being aware of cycles and the potency of our choices, both in our personal lives and in the wider world.

THINGS TO REMEMBER

1. Nature is full of fractal patterns.

2. Fractals are a common thread that runs from the quantum world, through nature as we know it, to the cosmic world.

3. Much of human life and nature is governed by cosmic cycles.

4. Much of human biology operates cyclically.

5. Nature impacts us in cyclic ways, so we get the sense that many of our life experiences repeat themselves.

6. Circumstances in life repeat themselves over time until we make different choices.

CHAPTER 2

UNDERSTANDING AND PREDICTING PATTERNS

'One of the key factors for me is understanding the world you live in, understanding what role you play in that journey.'

JAMES CAAN

Along with an understanding of the patterns and cycles in nature, and the patterns and cycles in our own lives, we need to know more about the world around us if we want to start to make significant and lasting changes to our lives.

Specifically, if you want to achieve something, it helps if you know more about the arena you'll be achieving in – your personal world. If you understand how this, and the wider world, work, you can predict how they may change in the future and see how you may need to change yourself too, to move *with* a cycle rather than *against* it.

The first step to understanding your personal world is to decide *what it is* that you want to understand. Once you've done that, you can then begin to gain knowledge about it. And you can do this through research and asking questions.

Research and Asking Questions

'If you don't know something, one of the beauties of life is the simple way of resolving that problem: just ask the question.'
JAMES CAAN

British business guru and philanthropist James Caan knows the value of asking questions to gain an understanding of his personal world. When he doesn't have the information he needs to get on, he turns to a simple solution: *'Ask somebody who does know,'* he advises. *'If you have the ability to do that, it is quite incredible how your journey can change drastically just by being able to ask the question.'* James believes we can achieve so much more in life if we are prepared to ask the right questions. However, many people prefer to work it all out on their own, as James observes. *'They don't ask enough questions to strengthen their ability to craft the journey for themselves,'* he says.

Asking questions is a powerful tool for understanding your personal world, and the more questions you ask, the better you'll get at it. You don't need to know *everything* about where you want to go in life, you only need to ask how to get there. As James says, *'One of the things I have learned is that life is not necessarily about being an expert on the answer, but it is about being an expert on the question.'* And having no previous experience of something doesn't mean you can't attempt it, either. You just need the right information. When you get that, and act on it, you'll be surprised how much you can achieve.

Asking questions enabled James to set up a charitable foundation, which has had a huge impact on the lives of thousands of people. The foundation is in the process of rebuilding a village in Pakistan, where 20 million people lost their homes and livelihoods after the floods of 2010. *'Rebuilding an entire village, with all the challenges of engineering and power and so on, has been an incredible challenge,'* James says. *'But I am delighted that I had the conviction of my own beliefs to do something, despite the fact that I had no idea whether I could or not.'*

In order to achieve the foundation's goal, James asked questions and listened to the answers he received, taking guidance where it was necessary, and this helped him to solve many problems and achieve things much more quickly than if he'd tried to work everything out for himself.

Emmy award-winning composer and musician Peter Buffett stresses the importance of listening carefully to the answers to the questions you ask in your attempts to understand your personal world. *'What I have learned specifically through my philanthropic work is if the real estate mantra is location, location, location, the philanthropic mantra is listen, listen, listen,'* he says.

Of course, we cannot accept everything we are told verbatim. We need to separate fact from opinion. The question is only the starting point on our journey. As James Caan puts it: *'It is very easy to blame the world, or something you've read. It is very easy to blame somebody who has told you something. I think what is important is having the ability to challenge some of that information, whether you have read it or have been told it. Just because you hear it or read it, doesn't mean it is fact. And this is how I think your ability to ask questions, to challenge information, makes you a stronger individual.'*

Acting on What You Learn

Jack Canfield gives us another example of how important research and asking questions is in our efforts to understand our personal worlds. A friend of his had noticed a decline in the number of people attending his seminars. He wondered what was going on and decided he could sit there and speculate, or go find out for himself.

'So he went to the marketplace and called all his students,' Jack recalls. *'He called more than 1,000 people and asked them whether they were still spending money on personal development. Most of the students said that they were, so he then asked them: "Well, you aren't spending it with us, so why not?"*

And the students replied: "Because we feel we know most of what you think already. We now need specific niche information, for example, how do you take this issue of responsibility and apply it to running a company, or how do you take this issue of the Law of Attraction and apply it to international trade?"

So, he went back and developed lots of new modules and now he is very successful again,' Jack says.

Rather than sit back and do nothing, Jack's friend placed high importance on understanding his world and took very seriously the idea that asking questions would help him to do that. After he'd interviewed a large number of his students, he discovered that people in his field wanted specific information that they could apply to their own struggles and directions in life, and he acted on it.

Of course, he might eventually have acquired this information without being proactive, without asking questions, but it would have come much later and by then, it might have been too late to save his business. But by taking action, he was able to transform his approach by research and asking questions.

Jack and his friend have come to understand a trend in the world: a pattern. *'People are going more and more to niche information on demand; when I want it, related to me specifically as supposed to something general,'* he says. *'It used to be we could go online and teach a seminar on something very broad, but today people have been exposed to the broad, now they want very specific information niched to their specific problem.'*

Jack is now able to serve up a helping of wisdom about paying attention to the trends around us: *'So, if you understand these trends, you can cooperate with them, and you can actually get ahead with them,'* he explains. *'I like the metaphor, "If you see the wave coming you can start paddling and you can surf the wave, but if you don't see the wave coming, you'll either miss it, or it will drown you."'*

Spotting Trends

Understanding patterns helps us to see a trend coming and get involved in the early stages, increasing our chances of success. Jack Canfield tells us how this allowed him to develop the niche series of books for which he and his friend and coauthor Mark Victor Hansen are famous: *'We found with the* Chicken Soup for the Soul *books that after we'd done the first book, and then a second helping, a fourth course, a fifth bowl, all of a sudden it was* Chicken Soup for the Woman's Soul, Chicken Soup for the Mother's Soul, Chicken Soup for the Working Mother's Soul, the Christian Mother's Soul. *The more we niched down, the more successful the books became, because people said, "Oh, that's for me." And so I think that's a trend in the world, people wanting that.'*

Jack also understands that products follow cycles, so by capitalizing on this and creating niche products, we can stay ahead of the wave. Seeking to understand your personal world can lead to quite staggering success, as Jack proves. The *Chicken Soup* series has sold around half a billion copies worldwide to date, helped by the fact that Jack and Mark understand the need to create niche books that feed the souls of people in specific life situations. They spotted the trend – the pattern.

Musician Peter Buffett explains how his father, the phenomenally successful businessman and philanthropist Warren Buffett, came to understand the patterns in the financial markets by researching the information available. *'He would read all these different periodicals and all these different publications from different sources,'* Peter recalls, *'because they gave him a picture he could work from. They were what allowed him to see patterns in the variety of places he got the information from.'*

So, if you research and ask questions, you can gain a much better understanding of your personal world. And, very often, you will notice that things happen in cycles. Being aware of this, and not resisting the cycles, can enable you to reinvent yourself, or your business, so that you stay on the crest of the wave, seemingly ahead of a cycle, and always making the best choices at the right time.

So these are the steps: decide what it is that you want to understand, and then research and ask questions about it.

From Crisis to Cooperation

'Crises often precede transformation and innovation.'
BARBARA MARX HUBBARD

When we look at the world right now, we can see that we are facing crises on an unprecedented, global scale: in our economies, in energy resources, in overpopulation and hunger, and in climate change. It seems that humanity faces crises cyclically. Take, for instance, weather patterns, many of which are cyclic. They often affect the availability of food in drought-prone countries, which often leads to shortages and even famine.

Extending this concept to the wider world, writer and educator Barbara Marx Hubbard encourages us to look at the crises we are facing as opportunities for us to create a better way of doing things. *'Problems are evolutionary drivers,'* she says, and suggests we can look at our own lives in these terms, too. *'This is true of your own life. It's driving you. You don't always respond, but if you do, you'll probably find you're going toward something more creative.'*

Our evolutionary history shows us that very often in our response to crises we tend to move toward something more creative: a better way of doing things. We learn to work together for the common good. Barbara Marx Hubbard draws on the teachings of evolutionary biologist Elizabet Sahtouris to explain that, *'when the species is young in evolutionary history, it tends to be competitive. It fights with itself, it overshoots its environment, and either it learns to cooperate with its environment, and other species, or it becomes extinct.'*

Working Together

In these terms, it would seem that we are a relatively young species in many ways; one that fights with itself and exhausts its environment, but these behaviors are no longer sustainable. We can see where we are right now: we are facing a Choice Point. We can cooperate with each other and find creative solutions to the world's problems, or we can make ourselves extinct.

Hope lies in the lessons of our evolutionary history, specifically in the way our ancestors learned to survive by cooperating with each other. As Barbara points out: *'We are actually the result of a species that learned to do that in some way.'* Otherwise we wouldn't be here. At this Choice Point, we need to learn to cooperate on a global scale, because doing so will ensure our survival.

It is in our nature to strive to survive and so, with this in mind, and with the current crises facing humanity, we can actually predict emerging global patterns, or trends, that are leading us toward greater cooperation. This is a new pattern that is emerging in the world as life seeks a way to continue, and it will undoubtedly become stronger.

Barbara says we should simply look for the direction nature would take in order to survive. *'The pattern you could see if you're in a town, or if you are dealing with any kind of shortage of goods, or you're dealing with what kind of car to drive, or how many babies to have... look at the pattern of this crisis that we're in, and then see which way would nature be moving.'*

And nature naturally moves toward cooperation. And from there, we learn to communicate.

From Cooperation to Communication

'Communication is huge, and the idea that something can happen over here and not be known halfway around the world in five minutes, that's over.' JACK CANFIELD

We live in an interconnected world, embedded within social networks in towns, cities, and nations. In order to cooperate with each other, we need to communicate. Through understanding this, we may be able to predict some of the natural patterns that will emerge in the future. As we move toward greater cooperation as a survival instinct, we also move toward greater communication to facilitate this.

And so, just as patterns of cooperation are emerging in the world, and will continue to do so in the future, we can predict the same for patterns of communication, too. We are already seeing patterns of greater, faster, and more efficient communication – from the Internet to cell phones. Barbara Marx Hubbard marvels at the speed with which this has happened. *'Who would have guessed that these little cell phones met a need, a pattern, for the desire to communicate, so that there are now 4.1 billion people on the planet who you can reach through a cell phone, and who can reach each other. That's a pattern of desire to connect,'* she says.

Barbara relates this phenomenon to the natural direction of nature. *'What I do with those patterns is I place them in a larger picture,'* she explains, *'and that goes back to a pattern in nature for the whole planetary intelligence system to be connecting; via media, via Internet, via cell phone, via all these different modes of communication. There is a pattern in there.'* She invites us to relate this pattern to our own lives, too. *'What does that pattern mean applied in your relationship, or in your village or town?'* she asks, adding: *'You can see that you're part of a larger pattern.'*

A Connected Future

So, we can think of cooperation and communication as emerging trends, or patterns, that will grow even stronger in the future. We can even consider that the solutions to the problems in our lives, in our businesses, in our communities, in our world, can be found in cooperation and communication. We can also look around us and see where greater cooperation and communication are already taking place, and perhaps move ourselves into these patterns if we wish to move forward in, say, our businesses, as these patterns are where much of the energy is going to be focused in the future. We can learn to surf the wave!

Nature always strives to survive, so we can predict that since nature naturally progresses toward cooperation and communication as survival modes, then any attempts to thwart them are not going to work, whether that is in our communities, in our businesses, or in our world. People naturally want to connect. And attempts to stifle that desire will be met with fierce resistance, as Jack Canfield observes. *'There are certain governments that are still trying to shut down cell phone services and control the Internet, but that's not going to last,'* he says. *'That is going to go away really quickly.'*

Connection is a biologically wired thing, with roots in the hormone oxytocin. It is the biological glue that holds us together in relationships, and ensures that we care for each other. It is the endogenous chemical force that causes us to crave connection with each other.[1] The oxytocin gene is one of the oldest in the human genome. It is around 500 million years old. It also ensures that empathy, compassion, and kindness are natural, inbuilt tendencies.

Empathy is the breeding ground for love and a willingness to help others. Bill Drayton believes that empathy is vital if we are to create a positive future in a fast-changing world. As the ways in which we connect and communicate multiply, it is crucial that we are still able to relate to, and understand, each other. *'If you don't have empathy,'* Bill says, *'you can't really understand all the people around you. Empathy is the foundation that allows you to be a good team player.'*

Our ability to empathize will become very important in the future, because it is from empathy that we are moved to help each other and to seek solutions to make the world a better place. As Bill points out: *'Once people have these tools, there is no question that they will want to express love and respect in action; they will want to be a contributing part of society.'*

From the Love of Power to the Power of Love

'When I really look at different people, I am amazed at the great gift of having a strong heart's desire to express and to give. It's a gift.' **BARBARA MARX HUBBARD**

As we cooperate and develop technologies to communicate, we will rapidly see where good things are happening in the world, but we will also easily learn where there are injustices. Due to our natural tendency for compassion, we will want to correct these, and so another pattern that we might predict is an aspect of the cooperation pattern – a focus on social causes.

There is a rapid growth occurring in social entrepreneurship, where entrepreneurs use their skills to create a positive social change in the world. Bill Drayton believes social entrepreneurship is approaching a tipping point. He says: *'In the last three months I have written five prefaces to new books on this subject – this is not what I was doing a few years ago. And virtually every university now has major programs that have come up in the last five years on social entrepreneurship. At Harvard Business School, of all places, social enterprise is now bigger than marketing and finance among the students.'*

In business, too, we are seeing an increase in the number of people who want the company they work for to support social causes. And with greater communication, and the transparency that comes with it, people are also much more aware of what companies are doing, and, in particular, what they are *not* doing. So a pattern is emerging in which people are less likely to support companies that exploit people, or the environment.

We can also predict a pattern of people looking for more honesty and transparency in the wider world. Jack Canfield says: *'We see all this investigative reporting, we see WikiLeaks out there and people are hungry to know what's really true. And more and more, I think, transparency and openness and honesty and telling the truth are a big trend we are going to see in corporations, in the media, in relationships, and in the government, hopefully. People get upset when they don't have that, so we know that if anything is upsetting you, it is telling you there is a need that humanity has right now that is not getting fulfilled.'*

We Can All Make a Difference

Politicians and business leaders who try to block this in an attempt to maintain their own power are diminishing in their influence. Those who promote it, on the other hand, are increasing in theirs. As Barbara Marx Hubbard points out: *'At the heart of power, some people's desire is to use that power and to control and to manipulate and win. But because we're hitting a planetary crisis of overgrowth, that desire to win and control, I think, is going to be ever less effective. And the desire to connect and create toward a shared vision is going to be ever more attractive.'*

Barbara is clear about the challenge facing the world's leaders today. *'I think you find that many leaders now at the corporate level, in the technological world, in the religious world, are thinking how they can shift from that old structure they were in toward their own creativity,'* she says. *'And I have faith that this is a very powerful force now.'*

And we can all contribute to this change, as Barbara explains: *'Where we're at is that there are Choice Points being made in every sector of human society, in every field. And the key to making the shift would be to identify the Choice Points, to see where positive choices are being made, to connect those Choice Points and communicate, so the average person sees it is possible for us to have this kind of future.*

'And then for each person to think: "I've got some part in that, no matter what level I am. If I have a simple life, I have the possibility of being part of a planetary shift by doing better what I already do." But if you have a lot of freedom to make choices, as many people do, with education and freedom to move and freedom to communicate, then the Choice Points are obvious and the positive solutions are necessary. I think that can then affect the whole planet.'

Each one of us can make a positive difference then because we all play a part in this world, however small. When we embrace the power of love rather than the love of power, then the difference we make can be a powerful one.

THINGS TO REMEMBER

---

1. Doing research and asking questions are good ways to understand your world.

2. We need to *act* on what we learn from research and asking questions.

3. Crises precede cooperation.

4. We need to cooperate to survive.

5. We need to communicate to cooperate.

6. Cooperation and communication will be strong patterns in the future.

7. A solution to many of our problems is to exercise the power of love over the love of power.

In the next part of the book, you will learn a little more about how reality is constructed so you can begin to fully appreciate just how much of an effect each of your choices has. You will be inspired to find your own purpose, too, and learn how to align it with the patterns that are currently emerging in the world.

PART 2
ALIGN YOUR PURPOSE

CHAPTER 3

INFORMATION EXCHANGE

'Information is really the fundamental building block of the universe.'

VLATKO VEDRAL

Imagine you are floating down a wide river in a canoe. You have a paddle with you. Now this is a metaphorical canoe because it represents you, and the river represents your reality. Your life is where your canoe floats. On the whole, the river is flowing forward, but there are also currents running within it. If you paddle your canoe toward a particular current – if you align yourself with it – you'll get in the flow of the current and it will take much less effort to move downstream. If you choose not to align with the current, though, you'll have to work a lot harder.

In this part of the book we explain how our lives flow with much greater ease when we align ourselves with a current. Or to continue with the language we've been using – when we align ourselves with a fractal pattern or cycle.

We have choices in our lives. We can choose to align ourselves with a pattern. It could be a new way of doing things, or it could be a new technology. It doesn't even need to be something new, but it helps if it is something that is in harmony with a lot of other people. If we align with a pattern and the pattern scales up, so to speak, when a cycle comes around in a bigger way, we are caught up with it.

To fully understand this concept, and to be able to use it positively to better ourselves and the world, we first have to understand a few things about the nature of reality. And in order to do that, we need to briefly explore a branch of the science of Information Theory.

Information Everywhere

'I think now there is a new picture emerging, and I think we should really substitute matter and energy with a more fundamental concept, and in this case I think information would be much more appropriate.' **Vlatko Vedral**

Imagine you are floating in space and that the only sense you have is hearing. You cannot feel or perceive anything in any other way. You are new to reality but you want to understand what it is, so you use the sounds you hear to develop your understanding.

You are close to a road on which cars are whizzing along. Of course, you don't know it's a road because you are new to reality, nor do you know what a car is. All you are aware of are periodic 'whoosh' sounds thanks to your sense of hearing. So you conclude that reality is made up of pulses of 'whoosh' sounds. You might even work out a mathematical equation that can predict when the next whoosh will come. But this is not the *whole* picture of reality. It is information that you have gained *about* reality, using your sense of hearing.

Now imagine that you develop the sense of sight. All of a sudden, the whoosh sounds take on a new meaning. You can now see they are caused by colored 'tubes' (cars) that rush along some sort of gray track (road). And you now understand that the whoosh sounds weren't fundamental to reality. The colored tubes on the track are reality, at least as far as you can conclude from your two senses. And you can see there are three different colors. The majority of the tube is in what you decide to call 'red.' There are bits you can see through (windows) so you call those 'clear,' and there are four parts at the bottom (tires), which you define as 'black.'

But again, this is not a *complete* picture of reality. You don't really know the innermost workings of reality. You only have information *about* reality. Nature presents itself to you in different ways depending on which sense you use to experience it. The commonality in both of your experiences is 'information.'

Now imagine that you are next gifted with the sense of touch. You reach out and touch one of the tubes, which has stopped for a moment. You learn that it is hard. Touching other parts of it, you find that it has a variety of different textures. You can feel metal, glass, and rubber, and so you conclude that these three textures are fundamental building blocks of reality.

But again, you are not receiving the *full* picture of reality. You are merely receiving information *about* reality. So, rather than concluding that reality is made up of whoosh sounds, three colors, and three textures, all you can really say is that you have information *about* reality. All you can *ever* get is information *about* reality. You may in time develop another sense that gives you even more information, but in each case, what you gain is information.

So we can think of reality as pieces of information. And as we are also part of reality, we need to include ourselves in the picture. We must think of ourselves as pieces of information, and everything that we think, say, and do in our lives as pieces of information, too.

It is from this position that we work in this part of the book, as we explain how we interact with the world around us.

Information as a Blueprint

Now let's broaden our understanding a little more. Information also determines form. Think of the human body. Information held in DNA determines the shape of the body. It governs the shape of its cells, the length of its limbs, the color of its eyes and hair, and even its size. Information is what the cells use to join together to create a human being.

Information also underlies a phenomenon known as 'emergence,' in which order emerges out of something seemingly chaotic. An example is the way in which a beautiful snowflake pattern emerges out of the random tumbling of ice crystals through cold air.

In physics, fields of energy create matter, but information determines the form that the matter takes. We can think of information as like instructions: the blueprint that tells energy which form to take. So we can say that the reality we know is made of energy and matter, but information determines its form.

But how much can we interact with reality? We know that we are part of cycles in nature, but can we actually *change* things within these cycles? It's an empowering idea and, in fact, we do it all the time. We affect the information around us that determines what happens in our lives because we exchange information with it. Let's return to our canoe metaphor. When we align with a current we exchange information with it in that the paddle and the hull of the canoe mix with the water. Exchanging information with a pattern is like becoming part of the 'vibe' of that pattern.

Of course, this is plain common sense and we don't need to go through life thinking about the language of information. But it *is* useful to think about it when we want a deeper understanding of our more subtle relationship with the reality around us, and especially when we want to learn how to 'shape' this reality to change our lives and positively impact the world.

One Big Matter

'So everything is energy that we have. And the energy is arranged in certain structures in space and time. And all this arrangement of energy is carrying information about itself.'
Dr. Rainer Viehweger

The patterns and cycles in nature act like currents in a river, guiding some of the directions we take, often unconsciously. We can decide to paddle our canoes in directions of our own choosing on this metaphorical river. But on a deeper level, our choices also have far-reaching effects because we exchange information with everything around us.

Think of a spider's web. Now imagine that every person on the planet is a node on that web, with its strands connecting them. Then imagine that this web is so big that it connects not just all of us, but *everything* in the universe. If such a thing existed, then every choice that each of us made would create vibrations – ripples or waves – on the web that would be felt everywhere and by everyone. In this way, we would constantly be in communication with the whole universe, exchanging information and energy through the vibrations we create, and also those that we feel. Each choice we made would be information that would ripple outward, interacting with the rest of the web.

Although such a web doesn't physically exist, the science of quantum mechanics does suggest that we are all intimately connected, so we can think of the spider's web as a simple model for the purposes of picturing how we interact with the world around us. The term used in quantum mechanics to describe this interconnectedness is Entanglement. Subatomic particles (protons, electrons, quarks, etc.) can be *entangled* with one another in such a way that it is possible to imagine there is some sort of strand connecting them.

Research into Entanglement began after Einstein published a paper with fellow physicists Podolsky and Rosen that is now referred to as the EPR (Einstein-Podolsky-Rosen) paper. Their work was actually an attempt to pick some holes in quantum mechanics because the theory and equations of the time were telling physicists that one subatomic particle could somehow be caught up in the reality of another, no matter how far apart the two of them were. In other words, if we were to 'touch' one of a pair of particles, the other would instantaneously react to the touch, even if it was in a distant galaxy, trillions of miles away.

Einstein felt that quantum theory must be incomplete because in his mind, such a thing was impossible. He coined a famous description of it as 'spooky action at a distance.' But research has now confirmed beyond all doubt that this 'spookiness' is for real. Entanglement is here to stay.

Everything is Connected

Vlatko Vedral, professor of quantum information theory at Oxford University in the UK believes we are constantly exchanging information with the universe and so we are, by nature, entangled with it. *'It is really this phenomenon of Entanglement that makes all the objects that have interacted somehow interlink together and makes it impossible for us to look at them as individual objects,'* he says. *'We should really take them as one big matter.'*

Entanglement can be explained in simple terms: humans give off heat, which carries information that tells nature about our physiological state. If we've been exercising our bodies will give off more heat. This information interacts with nature around us – the molecules in the air close to us are warmed. Thus we are entangled with nature. We interact (or exchange information) with it, and affect it.

Of course, our effect on the reality immediately around us is much greater than our effect on, say, the solar system, because we exchange much more information with our surroundings than we do with that. But in a fundamental sense, it is impossible to think of ourselves as *separate* from our surroundings, or from each other, because of this information exchange. We are entangled, as Dr. Viehweger explains: *'The oscillations [vibrations] of our body and the oscillations [of the chair] that we sit on will communicate with each other because they are the same protons and the same electrons.'*

If we take the information exchange idea a little further, we can actually think of ourselves and the entire universe as one thing. *'That means that anything that exchanges information with its environment, and that is true for everything in the universe, including us humans, becomes inevitably actually entangled with the environment,'* says Vlatko Vedral. The point is, we are intimately connected in deeper and much more fundamental ways that we ever imagined, and that as we exchange information with reality, it's as if we 'speak' with it.

It is this capability that allows us to shape our lives for the better, and even to tip the scales of the world in favor of cooperation and peace. Also of significant importance is the fact that we exchange information with many fractal patterns – we affect them and they affect us. So at a fundamental level, aligning with patterns is all about exchanging information with them.

Interacting with Information

'That's really what's mind-boggling about quantum physics: that our input as physicists, namely what we decide to measure, seems to affect the response of nature at the most fundamental level.' VLATKO VEDRAL

Now let's return to our three senses analogy and explore a little more about how we shape some of the circumstances in our lives, and also how reality influences us. It was once thought that atoms were the fundamental, indivisible units of nature. That mantle has since been passed to subatomic particles, but you may now see that information is actually more fundamental than them, because information determines how a particle shows itself.

In an experiment that forms one of the cornerstones of quantum physics, scientists fire particles at two slits in a plate. If they are studying the path of the particles, then they find that, just like bullets from a gun, each particle goes through one slit.

But in a strange twist, if they perform the experiment differently, this time not following the path of the particle (bullet), it actually goes through *both* of the slits at the same time. The particle, or bullet, now seems to be a wave, just as ripples on the surface of water could spread through two gaps in a fence. If we watch or 'observe' the particles, they go through a single slit, but if we don't watch them, they go through both slits at the same time. This is known as the 'observer effect.' Essentially, we have two different types of experiment (or senses), which produce two different descriptions of reality.

In other words, a choice that we make regarding how to perform the experiment determines how nature presents itself, just as we could rely solely on our sense of hearing or our sense of sight.

There is a line of thought that says that since the nature of reality therefore depends on our observations, then we must be the sole creators of everything. But, according to Vlatko Vedral this is not the case. There is *'nothing at all special about humans,'* he says. Observation doesn't need eyes and ears. Observation is really just about the exchange of information. If information is exchanged, then there is an observation.

We are therefore not the only observers – in fact all particles in the universe are capable of observing each other, just as two ants on an anthill can observe each other. All they need to do is exchange information, which they do all the time. So nature exists independently of whether we are observing it or not. And patterns and cycles exist, regardless of whether we're aware of them or not.

It's Give and Take Between Destiny and Free Will

This is important to our thesis that cycles and patterns affect us *regardless* of whether we're aware of them or not, and that life is not the blank canvas that some of us believe it is. We are not the sole creators of our reality, then, but neither are we purely at the mercy of patterns and cycles. It's all about information exchange. If we change our focus – the information we put in – we get a different result.

Some people feel they have no control over their lives, that events, patterns, and cycles determine everything that happens to them; others feel they are firmly in the driver's seat, creating everything. But we're suggesting that it's a bit of both. So mastering life is about appreciating patterns and cycles and choosing to align with *some* over others, which we will explore throughout the remainder of this book. And aligning really comes down to the exchange of information.

When we exchange information with a pattern, for instance, we resonate with it and thus become linked, or aligned with it, going with the current for as long as we continue to exchange information with it. If we change our focus, then we can exchange information with a *different* pattern and align with that instead. This is how we change direction in life.

The more information we exchange with any part of our life, the more we become *entangled* with it. To use another analogy, it's as if we stitch ourselves into the pattern in a tapestry. Whatever happens to the tapestry happens to us, too. We can also think of it as like drawing a picture on a balloon. When we inflate the balloon, the picture expands. We call this (inflation of the balloon) the 'scaling up' of a pattern, for that is what fractal patterns do. They repeat themselves in bigger and bigger ways. They scale up but they are the same on larger scales. So if we align with a pattern, we go with it as it scales up over time.

In summary then: we are all connected. The entire universe is connected. And we 'speak' to this connection, drawing to us from an ocean of different patterns those that our thoughts and actions are aligning with (exchanging information with) – just as if we are steering our canoe into a current. The canoe is caught in the current because it is exchanging information with the current.

How Your Mind Influences Your Reality

'Our inner experiences, thoughts, feelings, emotions, and beliefs, are the language that speaks to the stuff that connection is made of.' GREGG BRADEN

At first, the thought of aligning with a fractal pattern or a cycle conjures up the idea that we need to physically *do* something – but we believe we can align with them not only through our actions, but with our thoughts, emotions, and beliefs too.

Our thoughts, emotions, and beliefs govern much of our behavior, so we can align with fractal patterns by making choices and physically moving our life *into* the cycle. Or, to use our river analogy, we use our paddle to steer our canoe into the current. But on a less obvious, but important, level our thoughts, emotions, and beliefs might also directly exchange information with the reality around us.

Our conscious awareness directly interacts with a pattern when we think of it. Imagine you want to be a carpenter. As you start to gather ideas and insights about carpentry, in one sense your mind is already aligning with a carpentry pattern as it receives information about the subject from books, courses, TV, etc. And as more information is received, you start to consciously and unconsciously look for more information about carpentry, and start thinking about it, picturing yourself working as a carpenter. And so you begin to exchange information with the carpentry pattern in your mind and align with it. And as you start to create things with wood, you exchange yet more information as you add to the carpentry pattern.

'Speaking' from the Heart

Now consider it in another way. Our thoughts and emotions generate brainwaves, which carry information about our mental goings-on. Brainwaves are electrical and magnetic in nature and so they interact with, and thus exchange information with, the reality around us.

It seems entirely likely that our brainwaves are entangled with each others, exchanging energy and information. We even propose that if many people hold the same idea in their minds there will be some harmonization of their brainwaves. And so if thousands of people are aligned with an idea, then we can align with them simply by holding the same idea in our minds. And if a pattern that was in harmony with many people is scaled up, then we could find ourselves changing with it in some way as we continue to exchange information with it.

Gregg Braden believes that we also interact with reality in this way, using our emotions like an amplifier to boost our connection to it. The heart, he says, helps us to interact with reality. *'The heart creates an electrical field that is about 100 times stronger than the brain's. But the magnetic field of the heart is about 5,000 times stronger than the magnetic field of the brain. And this gives completely new meaning and context as to why human emotion has the power it does to affect our physical reality.*

'We live in a world of electrical and magnetic stuff,' he continues. *'This quantum field, the matrix, whatever name we choose to give it – some physicists call it the mind of God – whatever the stuff is that holds everything together, electrical and magnetic fields make up a large portion of that stuff in our physical world. I think it is no coincidence that you and I were born with an organ in our bodies that is designed to communicate with this stuff.'*

So we propose that on a very subtle, yet real, level our thoughts and emotions are entangled with reality because they continually exchange energy and information with it through the electrical and magnetic fields generated by our brains and hearts. So in one way we create the circumstances around us by our actions, but in other ways we see patterns in our lives that have our personal stamp on them: circumstances, people, and events that reflect our thoughts and emotions because they are in some ways generated by them.

Conscious Creation

In this unseen, and rather esoteric way, then, it is possible that our thoughts and emotions actually *create* our personal realities to some extent. Gregg is convinced that it is also the quality of our mental focus that determines how well we interact with reality (exchange information with it), and how consciously we shape our circumstances in line with what we want in life. *'The controversy is to what degree we influence the electrical and magnetic stuff,'* he says. *'The answer to that is where the science is having a difficult time because it is all determined by the quality of the focus that we place within ourselves, between our heart and our brain. This is where the electrical and magnetic patterns are generated.'*

In other words, if you have a goal and then generate the feeling of the completion of that goal in your heart, then you link your brain and heart so that both are focused on the same idea and not pulling in opposite directions. In this way, the thought of your goal interacts with the world around you, exchanging information with it through the electrical and magnetic field of the heart.

Gregg then expands a little on how he believes the process works. *'We make a choice and we claim that choice in our hearts,'* he says. *'We begin the choice in our brains as an idea with a relatively weak electrical and magnetic field and then we amplify that choice through our hearts. We claim it and the feeling is as if the choice has already come to pass, the healing has already happened or the abundance is already present.'*

A similar idea is held to be true by many of the world's ancient wisdom and spiritual traditions. Some wisdom traditions tell us that if we want to achieve our dreams in life, heal our bodies, achieve success, or make the world a better place, we need to hold the image of these dreams in our minds and feel the emotion that we would feel if we had already achieved them. Even though there is no empirical evidence in science to back it up, the belief that our thoughts create our reality in this way has been built up over thousands of years through personal observations and experiences.

Gregg also says that the patterns that we create mix with and align with patterns around us, exchanging information with them, and that a consequence of this is that life becomes easier. *'When those patterns fit well into the existing patterns,'* he explains, *'then we feel that there is a harmony and a flow and an ease.'*

It's Your Mind That's Waving

'You could say that objects don't really exist independently in their own right until they have exchanged information with other objects, which then confirms this existence, if you like. If you phrase physics in this relational way, then it really starts to sound like some of the ideas of emptiness in Buddhism. So there is no underlying reality other than relationships between different objects.' **VLATKO VEDRAL**

Everything we do, whether we are aware of it or not, in some small way affects everything else in the world. This is what Entanglement tells us. And as Vlatko Vedral says, it is impossible to think of things as separate and that we should really take them as *'one big matter.'* Everything exists in relationship with everything else. If you change one thing, other things also change.

This belief is quite similar to those that have been espoused by spiritual and wisdom traditions for thousands of years. One of the central ideas of these traditions is 'oneness' – the belief we are all connected, that all things are part of a single essence, or intelligence, and that as we change ourselves, we find that change reflected throughout our world.

You might have noticed some of the parallels between quantum physics and the teachings of some of the spiritual and wisdom traditions. Both the spiritual and the quantum mechanical are captured in a simple story relayed by the Chinese Zen master Huineng, who lived from 638–713. It is retold here by Vlatko Vedral:

'Two kids are observing a flag waving in the wind. One of them says, "Look how nice it is that this flag is waving." And the other replies, "It is not the flag that is waving, actually, it is the wind that is blowing it." The Zen master is passing by and overhears the conversation. He turns to the kids and says: "No, both of you are wrong. It is neither the wind nor the flag. It is your minds that are waving."'

Vlatko says that 'the story could be retold in scientific language almost word for word,' as it reflects different, but valid, interpretations of quantum mechanics.

Cycles and patterns exist in nature and they act like the wind. So from this perspective, the wind waves the flag. But your mind also generates information that can alter your reality subtly and through your actions so the flag waves *because* of you. In this way, it is your mind that is doing the waving. In experimental physics, the mind waving can be thought of as us choosing to carry out our experiments in a particular way, so that we get a particle or a wave, and so create our reality.

This is one of the reasons why quantum physics is attractive to those who seek a spiritual, holistic, understanding of life. They are interested in its philosophical implications. In fact, some of the early pioneers of quantum mechanics had a spiritual view of life. Max Planck, one of the founding fathers of quantum mechanics, claimed, 'There is spirit permeating the universe.'

Oneness

The scientific and spiritual worldviews agree on the unity of the universe – the 'oneness' – but they use different languages to describe the concept. In quantum physics, this sense of oneness is through Entanglement. In spirituality, some form of practice helps us to expand our sense of self and then we begin to feel an intuitive and emotional connection with all of humanity, with nature, and with all things. At this point, all ideas of you, me, or anything being separate vanish, leaving behind only the deep and profound experience of oneness.

In this state we feel a deep sense of the patterns around us, and feel that we can align with any of them at will with our thoughts and emotions, as if they are tentacles that emanate from us and can wrap around anything we wish. Spiritual teachings have taught us for thousands of years that the state of oneness is accompanied by love and a deep sense of peace, and so when we think and act from love, we align with the oneness of the universe. We understand the far-reaching consequences of our minds, and sense the power of the entire universe within us.

A diverse range of people hold such a spiritual, interconnected view of the world, despite the beliefs of mainstream science. Britain's Dr. Scilla Elworthy, founder of the Oxford Research Group and three times Nobel Peace Prize nominee, describes her idea of oneness as being part of a much greater whole and says: *'I am thrilled to have the opportunity to be that part, and that the part I play does have an effect. I don't know what it is really, but I know that the one little cell does affect all the rest, just as a butterfly flapping its wings in Costa Rica can alter the weather in Japan. So what each person does and says, and even thinks, matters in the whole.'*

And Alison Pothier, the former chief operating officer of an international investment bank, expresses her spiritual sentiments with the words: *'For me, oneness means that everything outside of me is part of me; that everything I see is me and that I am not only observing it but I am it. It is my dream. So there is nothing that I am not, and there is nothing that is not me. That is oneness to me.'*

THINGS TO REMEMBER

---

1. We can think of reality as pieces of information.

2. We are connected (entangled) with all of this information.

3. Our choices affect the reality around us.

4. There is an interplay between destiny and free will.

5. We can align with patterns through our thoughts, emotions, beliefs, and actions.

6. Aligning with a pattern is about exchanging information with it.

CHAPTER 4

ALIGNING SENSIBLY

'When the pattern doesn't fit well with existing and natural patterns, or the patterns as we know them at that time, then that is when we might find things difficult in our lives.'

GREGG BRADEN

Many, many patterns exist around us. Some are created by nature, others by our collective behavior and intentions – there are, for instance, established patterns for teaching, science, religion, engineering, and many other disciplines, as well as the new branches that grow out of these. Other patterns are less obvious.

We don't always notice the patterns around us, but our individual lives are the sum of the interaction of all the patterns of energy and information that we are aligned with, both consciously and unconsciously. Life is the journey of all the currents we travel on. If, for example, you are always thinking of drawing, then you will be aligned with a pattern of art, and will therefore be exchanging information and energy with it.

When we align with a different pattern though – perhaps through a different mental focus, emotion, or action – we change the quality or experience of our lives, just as if we had steered our canoe into a new current. And when we are part of that current, reaching a particular destination requires less effort than if we tried to reach that destination without it. Think of it this way: if you are completely aligned in your heart and mind with an accountancy pattern, you'll find it much more difficult to paint a masterpiece.

If we don't align with a pattern, we don't have access to its influence. That's the bottom line. It's like we miss the current and have to paddle by ourselves, which uses up much more energy. Achieving what we want in life is about shifting our awareness – the direction of our minds and our actions – to sync with particular patterns. To put it another way, aligning with a pattern is like tuning in to a station on a radio. Just as we tune in to the station by turning the dial, so we can turn the dial in life by changing our mind or our actions. Numerous other radio stations – and patterns – still exist around us, but we are not tuned in to them.

The same kind of thing happens on a global scale. There are numerous fractal patterns around us that are a consequence of our collective thinking, decisions, words, actions, and interactions, and these aggregate into collective patterns, like radio stations. In this way, our larger reality is consensual – it is the station we collectively tune in to as societies, cultures, and nations.

If you're not aligning with a pattern, it will be outside your experience. This doesn't mean it doesn't exist, of course. It exists in other people's experiences. It's just that it's highly unlikely to exist for you.

Many Things Are Possible, but Not Everything Is Likely

'If we want to reach a goal it would be very useful to know the rules about how matter likes to be arranged... Because if we use the ways matter would like to go by itself, we don't need so much energy to do it.' DR. RAINER VIEHWEGER

The universe is full of matter, but as we discovered earlier, it is in 'clumps' and there are vast areas of empty space between the clumps. The clumps of matter (galaxies) are where most of the 'business' is being done, so to speak. If we were to travel through space we would go through long stretches of time and space devoid of any matter at all, and then pass through short bursts of time and space when there is lots of matter.

We've learned that the universe can be considered as information, that it is fractal in structure, and that there could be a fractal connection between the quantum world and the physical world. We also know that we exchange information with, and are entangled with, the universe. So we propose that the 'texture' of our life events will therefore have the same texture as space.

The Texture of Life Events

Are you familiar with the expression 'You wait ages for a bus and then three come along at once?' It's a popular cliché, but our life experiences tell us that there is an element of truth to it. Sometimes we can be looking for a new job without success, and then we are offered two or three in a short space of time. Or we can be striving to succeed in one of our goals and finding that nothing much is working and then we have a golden period, where successes happen one after another. Similarly, we sometimes experience a 'cluster' of negative events around the same time.

In each of these examples, it's as if we have moved from an empty part of space into an occupied part – a bubble, or a 'cluster' of matter. So given that our life events have the same texture as space, if our minds are aligned with what we want at these times, events will seem to conspire to help us. But if they aren't, events will seem to cluster together in a seemingly erratic way because they are just a product of the patterns that we are unconsciously aligned with.

At other times, when the pattern is in a stretch of empty space, very little seems to happen in our lives, and our efforts produce fewer rewards. Sometimes we may even feel as if we're swimming against the current. This is the nature of reality and these kinds of occurrences tell us there is a right or a best time to do things. There is a right time to act on a goal or a dream, for example, especially if you want to minimize your effort. There will always be times when the conditions are riper than others.

So, many things are possible for us, but this also means that not everything is likely. There are things that are simply more likely than others, and this is due to the 'shape' of the pattern in space and time that we align with – whether we are at a cluster of matter in space and time or at a large stretch of emptiness – and also whether we are aligned with the right pattern or not.

When we recognize this, changing things in our own lives becomes a lot easier.

Aligning with Harmonious Patterns

But what if you want to change things on a larger scale? What if you want to make a big difference in the world? A lot depends on whether what you want to change is harmonious with the needs and wishes of the people affected by it. If it *is* harmonious, you will have the collective buy-in from these people. This information creates a fractal pattern that you align with, and then change begins to happen.

If your change *isn't* harmonious, though, it is much less likely to work. Of course, you may well still succeed, but not without having to expend much more energy in the process. And when you stop pushing, there is a greater risk that things will unravel as they move back in the direction of what is best for (more harmonious with) the people concerned. This might seem a little disheartening, especially if you want to press ahead with your goals, believing that anything is possible. But, in a sense, anything is possible, as long as you align yourself with something harmonious. It's just that not everything is likely, especially if your goal isn't a harmonious one.

This knowledge is empowering because you can tune in to the harmonious patterns that *are* able to unfold in life; in other words, patterns that are being created or reinforced by large numbers of people – like patterns of communication and cooperation, for instance, which we explored in the first part of the book. And it does make sense, after all. Why wouldn't you want to build, create, or provide something that people need?

So, the more harmonious the pattern is – the more it is something that a lot of people want – the more easily it becomes real for you. And that can be enough to change your life and transform the world.

There's No Time Like the Present

In many ways, now is the time for us to pursue our goals, especially if they inspire us. When we feel inspired, when an idea captures or energizes us, we believe that this can be a sign that we are actually in sync (aligned) with a pattern that is already established, and which we are exchanging information with in some way, or even one that is ready to unfold because it serves a need.

The idea would have been born out of our interaction with the information in the reality around us. We can think of the idea as a new part of a fern leaf (a fractal pattern) as it grows. Because it is the leaf's destiny to grow that part, as long as we align ourselves with the pattern, take the actions we feel inspired to take, and be courageous when we have to be, we will flow with this destiny and become part of it as it grows. This is how many great leaps take place in technology. They happen at fertile times, when the conditions are right, just like the emergence of the new part of a fern leaf.

When we align with a new pattern, lots of things can happen very fast. We usually have to transform ourselves in the process, to keep pace, because we need to keep exchanging information with it as it grows. After a while, though, there are larger and larger gaps between big events, just as there are larger gaps between matter in the universe as we go from clusters (or 'clumps') of stars, to clusters of galaxies, to superclusters of galaxies.

So if we align with a fractal pattern very late, there might be long periods of time when there is actually little likelihood of any significant events. When this happens, we just have to work out what the harmonious patterns are most likely to be in the future and align with the new fractal pattern.

This is what Larry Page and Sergey Brin did when they created Google. They worked out that the most harmonious pattern was one where people could access information online almost instantly. Google was born and scaled up at a fantastic rate. It was as if a new part of the fern leaf started to grow. New ideas can seed trends, and then we get a new part of the fern leaf growing in a fractal fashion. The trend, of course, buys into a pattern that already exists. Microsoft,

Google, Facebook, and even the Internet itself are really just different arms on a much larger fern leaf, or fractal pattern, of communication.

Since reality is fractal based (consists of patterns), it is useful if we can recognize patterns that either exist at the moment or are likely to be harmonious with many people in the near future. When there are many people harmoniously interacting in the same way – thinking, wishing, intending, and acting around the same thing – we would expect the pattern to form faster and have more power.

Dancing in Time with the Music

'It's all about being in harmony and balance with the patterns in nature.' GREGG BRADEN

As we've learned, due to the structure of fractals in space and time, there are particular periods when things are more likely to happen. This is because of the information that gives the patterns their form. Some of that information is due to our collective, consensual needs; desires; and beliefs: So as ideas, needs, and desires start to emerge in our world, fractal patterns are seeded and begin to grow. If we align at this time, we can be carried along with the fractal as it grows.

This is how Bill Gates was able to revolutionize the computer industry when he did. He aligned with a massive fractal pattern that was arising from the combined desires of the thousands of people who were exploring computing at that time. But not only was he working at the right time in history, he was also in the right place. Fractal patterns can be localized in a particular place at a particular time, just as daybreak occurs in different places around the world at different times. For a number of reasons, conditions can be better in certain places.

The conditions were right for Bill Gates. He was attending the right school, he had access to the right equipment, and he also had the right friend in Paul Allen. He could not have created Microsoft in the nineteenth century, because the information, born out of the needs and desires to have personal computers, did not exist then. Similarly, if he had been born into a poor village in India and hadn't been educated, it's much less likely that he would have become one of the richest men in the world. Some might say that he was quite lucky. Maybe he was, but his passion, intelligence, interest, self-belief, and drive made up half the equation.

Mark Zuckerberg was also in the right place at the right time. The seeds of the Facebook idea were localized at Harvard University, where he was a student. He also had the right friend in Eduardo Saverin. But just like Bill Gates, he also had intelligence, a great passion, and self-belief. He also worked tirelessly to program and build Facebook, working almost round the clock in the early stages when lots of things were happening.

Understanding the Patterns in Your Life

'You repeat the same things over and over again.'
ROBERT E. QUINN

There are many patterns and cycles that play out in our lives, and we rarely notice them, but if we do pay attention to them, they can tell us a lot about ourselves. They can even lead us to new horizons of self-understanding, making it easier to transform our lives in whatever way we choose.

Because of the natural oscillatory (vibratory) nature of reality, natural cycles (and those created by others and by society) act like a cyclic wind upon us, sometimes playing us like a musical instrument, just as we might take cyclic breaths to play a flute. And so the tune we play is oscillatory. In the same way, the information content of our minds is met by these cycles and so the tune of our life experiences is of cyclic events that repeat themselves until we change the information in our minds. Then we dance to a different tune.

Life's Persistent Patterns

If you take some time to examine your life, you might notice that your personal history is full of cycles. Do you tend to stay in a particular place or job for a short time and then move on, for instance? Is that a normal pattern for you? Or do you find that the same issue or challenge keeps cropping up in your life at different times and in different places?

If you pay close attention to the persistent patterns in your life, you will be able to see what it is that your thoughts, beliefs, and behaviour are aligning with. If you are aligning with a particular pattern, then the 'reality' of that pattern will persist in your experience for as long as you are aligned with it in your thoughts, emotions, beliefs, and actions – for as long as you continue to exchange information with it.

For instance, if you were bullied in the past and this was connected to your thoughts, fears, or beliefs, then as long as you hold the same ideas in your mind, you align yourself with the fractal pattern of bullying that exists in human experience. And so you might continue to experience bullying in one way or another, in varying guises, at school or college, with bosses at work, with authority figures, even with your partners.

Robert E. Quinn, professor of business and management at the University of Michigan in the US offers some simple advice for breaking out of cycles. He says we should change our emotions: *'You repeat the same things over and over again,'* he explains, *'causing everything to get worse. You get caught up in a vicious cycle. If you change the emotion, you change the opportunity structure; you do something new. You start to move into a virtuous cycle that picks you up.'*

Becoming Aware of Our Thoughts and Behavior

We can change our emotions by becoming fully *aware* of how we are feeling. With awareness, we don't get caught up in the situation, but are consciously aware that what we are feeling is an emotion. And in this way, we are no longer gripped by the feeling but are able to observe it, and ourselves, instead. This gives us the power to do something different – to break out of the cycle.

Cycles can repeat in many different ways, though, and not just as negative experiences. Any type of experience can repeat itself. Often, when we strive to make the same internal point to ourselves, it raises the same issues, as James Caan discovered. Many of James's early achievements were driven, in part, by the need to show his father what he was capable of doing on his own. He had been forced to leave home at 16, after a dispute with his father about joining the family business. James had refused to join it because he felt instinctively that he wanted to work for himself one day, just as his father had done. Over the next few decades, James had much success, but each achievement, or peak in a cycle, was in some way an attempt to demonstrate his worthiness to his father. This need was born out of a great admiration for the man, as James tells us:

'What I find quite staggering, when I reflect back, is to see a man who arrives in a country where he doesn't speak a word of the language. He can't read or write, so even arriving at an airport and finding his way without being able to read a sign or speak to someone... I find that incredible. And then to start a business with nothing and from nothing. My father was a huge inspiration for just showing what could be done if you were driven, if you were motivated. So I think he was clearly a role model, a mentor.'

As opportunities presented themselves to James over the years, each was met with this inner desire to prove his worth. *'Every day I became stronger and realized that I had to prove to my father that, you know what, I can make it and I will make it,'* he recalls.

In many ways, an awareness of your own patterns not only gives you an idea of the types of situations you might face in the future, but it can empower you to change yourself for the better. If it is a cycle that you don't want, then you can take some action to change it. You can do this by stepping back and observing yourself and then changing your mind, changing what you tell yourself, changing what you do, or even changing aspects of your environment. With awareness, and through different thoughts and actions, you can align yourself with something different – maybe a new movement or an empowering idea. And when you do this, your reality changes.

It's important to become aware of the contents of your own mind. If you have a goal, for instance, try looking at how you think about it, or the emotions you feel. You might realize that you're not giving as much attention to the stuff that you really want in life as you thought, but are giving plenty of attention to what you *don't* want. You are giving more attention to your goal's *absence*, in other words – to the situation you don't actually want to be in.

As a rule, we complain about stuff and talk about it with other people. But this behavior merely feeds the pattern that gave rise to it. We align with the patterns that we give our attention to, so when we give too much attention to stuff that's not in harmony with where we want to go, we move ourselves in that direction. And the chances are that we will repeat the pattern until we change, or until something gives, which can often be our health, especially if the pattern causes us stress. So it's very important to be mindful of ourselves.

Getting Out of a Negative Spiral

Another thing that occurs when we align ourselves with patterns that move us in the opposite direction from where we want to go is that we naturally get bad results in life and it becomes hard to break the cycle. Think of it like this: when people take an inert medication that they believe is a real medication, they can get better. This is called the *placebo* effect. But, similarly, if people believe the medication will do them harm, it can do that too. This is known as the *nocebo* effect. In both cases, what people believe governs the outcome.

In life, when we feel we're in a negative spiral, it is quite normal to believe that things will never get any better. But that belief actually reinforces the situation. On the other hand, it's easy to be happy when things are going well. And this is the placebo effect in life experience. You *expect* more things to go well and that expectation actually helps things to go well.

So how can we break a negative spiral? With awareness! The moment we recognize that our minds have aligned with a pattern that is making things worse for us, we can begin the process of freeing ourselves. Awareness of what is happening gives us that power. We can step back and observe, and in that space of awareness we are no longer participating. We are then able to change what we want to change.

Awareness can set us free because we understand that all we actually need to do is *change our minds*. Then we can align with a more harmonious pattern because we can exchange information with *that* instead.

So which patterns should you align with? If you want to move toward a goal in life, then you have to define it so that you have a direction. We explore this in the next chapter of the book.

THINGS TO REMEMBER

1. If we align with a pattern, we flow with that pattern.

2. Success is easier if we align with a pattern that is harmonious with the needs and desires of large numbers of people.

3. Some things are more likely than others. It depends on the patterns we are aligned with.

4. Life events cluster because life mirrors the fractal structure of the universe.

5. Events tend to repeat themselves until we do something different.

6. Being aware of a repeating pattern helps us to step out of it.

CHAPTER 5

IT'S ALL ABOUT THE PURPOSE

'I think there comes a point where our purpose and our alignment with our purpose become vividly clear. That's the point at which we take a deep breath and say: "This just feels absolutely right."'

JODI ORTON

If you want to align with patterns that can improve your life, or make a difference in the world, it helps if you know which patterns to align with. You need to have a sense of direction, otherwise you'll simply paddle your canoe aimlessly down the river, with no real idea of which currents to paddle into. But when you *deliberately* choose a current, you align with it with certainty, committing to it fully.

Having a purpose can invigorate us. It can lend meaning to our lives. It's the dominant intention of what we want to create in our lives and in the world around us. It is more than a goal – it's an extension of who we are. Goals flow out of our purpose and they serve it in many ways.

If you haven't found your purpose yet, then let your purpose be to discover it. And once you find it, the key is to align it with patterns that are harmonious with others, those that are in line with patterns that are emerging in the world.

So, the first real step in aligning your purpose is to define your purpose.

Define Your Purpose

'Having a sense of purpose, having that sense of clarity, is I think what brings out the best in you and enables you to do the things you really want to do. And I think finding your place in society, finding your place in the world, is absolutely key to this.' JAMES CAAN

Very often in our lives, circumstances and situations tease a purpose out of us, giving us a whole new meaning and direction. A new idea, a goal, or a passion can begin to burn brightly in our minds at these times, gripping us completely. Sometimes it can be so powerful that it sets the tone for the rest of our lives, almost like destiny.

When Scilla Elworthy was just 13 years old, she experienced what might be described as a calling. It was 1956 and she was sitting watching TV when footage of the Hungarian revolution came on. Russian tanks were rolling into Budapest and Scilla was horrified to see children her own age throwing themselves in front of the tanks. This was a defining moment for her. She rushed upstairs and started packing her suitcase.

Curious, her mother asked what she was doing and Scilla said she was going to Budapest because *'there is something very bad happening there and I have to go and help.'* Her mother told her that she shouldn't be so silly, but when Scilla burst into tears, her mother realized how much she genuinely cared about these people, so she resolved to give Scilla the opportunity to get some training so she could be of service to people who are suffering in the world.

When she was 16, Scilla went to work in a home for displaced people. Some of the residents were survivors of Auschwitz and Scilla says she often listened to their stories – when they would talk about them of course. Later, she worked in France in a camp for Vietnamese refugees set up after the Vietnam War, and from there she moved on to serve in an orphanage in Algiers during the Algerian Civil War. These experiences molded Scilla, building and strengthening her inner sense of purpose. *'They gave me an ineradicable taste of the suffering of people, particularly women and children, as a result of war, and that never left me,'* she says. *'Just this feeling that you have in your heart that you've in a way shared that experience, although in this life I hadn't been through it, but I really knew what it felt like. And there was no option but to try and help. There was no other option. That was quite clear.'*

British entrepreneur and philanthropist Richard Branson also found a sense of purpose early in life – he started on the path to entrepreneurship when he was just 15. The Vietnam War was raging at the time, and Richard was vehemently opposed to it. But students didn't have much say in those days, so Richard decided to take action: *'I thought maybe we could start a national magazine for young people, to give them a voice, and to campaign against issues we felt strongly about,'* he explains.

Richard didn't have an office, or many resources – *'I worked out of the school phone box and managed to sell enough advertising to cover the printing and the paper costs,'* he recalls. But this helped kindle his focus, and his desire to make the project a success. As things progressed, though, he was spending more and more time on the magazine, which didn't serve his schoolwork very well. Finally, his headmaster gave him a choice. He could either stay at school and not do the magazine, or leave school and do the magazine. *'So I said goodbye and headed off to do the magazine,'* Richard says.

This decision helped Richard to establish a direction in his life and fired a passion that led to his entrepreneurship, and eventually to his current focus on solving some of the world's problems, which you'll learn more about later in the book.

It was being poor as a child and homeless twice as an adult that enabled American entrepreneur and philanthropist John Paul DeJoria to find his purpose. When he started his business, John Paul Mitchell Systems, John Paul had to spend the first two weeks living in his car! But he believes that these experiences shaped his life and helped him to understand what it is like to be poor and hungry.

They also molded his purpose, which is to do things that make the world a better place, as he explains: *'As I walk into homeless shelters, as I walk into places that people need to eat, knowing that I'm able to help out, that is my destiny, to be able to have an abundance and change the world with it. And if the abundance wasn't there, I'd still try and do things that make the world a better place to live. That is my destiny. I'm living it. I'm having such a happy life doing it.'*

James Caan also met with circumstances that forced him to define his purpose. As we know, his father wanted him to join the family business, but he chose to follow his own instincts instead. *'I think there was no question that it was always at the back of my mind that my journey would inevitably be about setting up my own business,'* he says.

Purpose in Persistence

Barbara Marx Hubbard found her purpose by asking herself questions after a pivotal event that occurred at the end of World War II. She explains what happened: *'The United States dropped the first atomic bombs on Japan. I was 15 and it was a total shock to me because I thought everything we did could be good. And when I saw that we could destroy everything with our power, I began to question myself, and then I began to ask, "What is the meaning of the new* power of science, technology, and industry that's good?" and "Where is the human race going with this power that we want to go?" and "Do we have any positive images of the future?"'

It became Barbara's passion to find the answers to these questions. She began to research. *'I read through philosophy and I read through religion, to try to find where we thought we were going at the next stage of our power. And I found that nobody knew.'* Undeterred, Barbara became even more practical in her search. *'So I tried to go to college and ask the questions,'* she says, *'but you couldn't ask them because there was no subject on the future of humanity. I tried to join the Church, but you really couldn't ask: "How will we all be changed for real in this lifetime?"'*

Then an opportunity presented itself to her. *'My father knew Dwight Eisenhower,'* Barbara explains. *'It was 1952 and he had just been elected president. I was 22 years old and still asking the questions. So I was taken to the Oval Office on a courtesy visit. President Eisenhower was just going to say, "Hello," and then I was going to leave.*

'He was very charming; he looked at me and said, "Hello young lady, what can I do for you?" And I replied, "Mr. President, I have a question for you. What do you think is the meaning of this new power that is good? Where are we going with science, technology and industry?"

'Eisenhower looked startled, then shook his head and said, "I have no idea." And that's when it flashed into my mind:

"Then we'd better find out." That started me on my path.'
She had found her purpose!

Birke Baehr discovered his purpose at the tender age of eight. *'I was looking over my mum's shoulder one day when she was logging onto her email,'* he recalls, *'and I saw on a news feed that some university had found mercury in high fructose corn syrup. I knew what mercury was from all my friends saying, "Don't eat mercury, don't break your thermometer, it'll kill you."*

'I knew that corn was a food, but I didn't know what high fructose corn syrup was. So I asked my mum and she said it was a sweetener used in sodas. And right then, that was the moment that really got me started... I said to my mum, "I'm not going to drink sodas any more."'

That was the beginning of Birke's journey as an activist for sustainable food and agriculture. At the time, his dream was to be an NFL football player, but as he learned more and more about food and the environment, it became such a passion. Eventually, he said to his mum: *'I don't want to be an NFL football player any more, I want to be an organic farmer instead. That way I can make a bigger impact on the world.'*

Becoming a Mom

Jodi Orton describes how her purpose of being an adoptive and foster parent to special needs children became clear to her. *'It was always important to me, even as a youngster and as a young adult, to make sure that what I was doing mattered,'* she says. After graduating high school, Jodi went to nursing school and it was during her psychiatric rotation that she saw inside the 'locked ward'. From there on in, she says, she *'became enthralled with the entire world of psychiatric nursing, especially working with children.'* This area held more meaning for her than any other form of nursing.

Jodi continued with her psychiatric education into her early 20s. *'I was delving deeply into child development, and also finding a lot of interest in sign language. And the law, too,'* she recalls. *'It all seemed to come together, in a strange way. It was important to me that these kids had advocates.'* She was beginning to be drawn into the world of helping children with special needs.

Jodi and her then husband tried to conceive a child, but found out that they couldn't. Jodi, however, was undeterred. *'In evaluating myself and what I believed, I always knew that I'd be a mom. There was no doubt in my mind that I would be a mom. After a bit of mourning over that, and coming to terms with my infertility, I decided to move forward with adoption,'* she says.

Making the decision to adopt was a Choice Point for Jodi and one that would shape the rest of her life. Eventually, an opportunity presented itself for her to adopt two children from Russia. While in college, Jodi had studied the fall of communism and the quick rise in democracy in Russia. She was also aware of the sad plight of many Russian children and babies. She had gone to a library information meeting and learned that with the fall of communism, more than 300,000 children ended up in orphanages because the Church and the government were no longer able to care for them. *'I look back on that now and think there was definitely a reason for that. I absolutely believe that was my path. I knew there was something that was drawing me in that direction,'* she says.

International adoption was still very new in 1994, and Jodi discovered that the process was fraught with hurdles. But she still *'believed truly in doing a service to the children who had no homes.'* When all the paperwork was done, Jodi was handed a book with more than 300,000 names in it and told to pick one. *'I opened up the book and there were L.J. and Helena's names, right underneath each other, in the area of southern Russia where we wanted the children to be from, and with the ages that we wanted the children to be. We knew then that this was a sign we were where we were supposed to be at that time. We said, "Those are the two we want."'*

During the final stages of the adoption process, Jodi was sent a video, which she watched over and over again. She recalls the moment when she met her two children, L.J. and Helena, for the first time: *'I'll never forget the day... It was as if I was meeting two actors that I'd seen on the small screen forever and ever, and here I was touching them and smelling them. Here I was, holding two little children who would forever know me as their mother.'*

Both children had developmental problems. Helena was 11 months old at the time, but as Jodi recalls,

'Developmentally, she was a 3-month-old. She had never worn a diaper, much less been dressed in brand-new clothes. L.J. was paralyzed from the waist down and totally mute. And here were two little children who were now being fussed over; who were being shown toys that they had never seen before, and whose lives were about to change drastically and forever.' Jodi's earlier experience in psychiatric nursing had paved the way for her to be an ideal parent to these children. She had found her purpose.

Another Level of Parenthood

Shortly after the adoption, Jodi's marriage broke down. But she went on to study law and gained a qualification. She also got a new husband, with whom she would go on to adopt and foster many more children. *'We realized that we had amazing parenting skills, that the two of us together were an awesome team,'* she says. After settling into a new home in a new state, the couple decided to become foster parents and to make a difference in the lives of even more children. *'We had four in our home who were thriving, even with their disabilities and with their challenges. And so we knew that we could branch out, we knew we could reach out and make a difference in the lives of other children. During our time in Iowa, we did that more than 100 times.'*

During those years, Jodi's purpose grew stronger and she learned to fully appreciate the difference she and her husband were able to make in the lives of children who needed love. *'It became very clear to us, as children were flowing in and out of our home, that the role of foster parents, good foster parents, was to take in the kind of child that society couldn't handle; the kind of children that had been so scarred by society, and society's shortcomings, that no one but good foster parents could parent them.'*

At one stage she had to make a choice between continuing her career in law or devoting herself to being a full-time mother. She recalls the exact moment she made the choice: *'We had 11 children in our home and I still was trying to continue with the legal work. I remember the phone ringing and a client from Arizona was on the other end. He was very disappointed because I hadn't returned a phone call from three days previously. That was just not me. I prided myself on being efficient and getting my work done, and representing my clients to the best of my ability. It was at that point, and at that moment, that I really began to define my role as a mom in realizing that this had to be my role in life – that I couldn't be the best of both worlds all of the time.'*

Just two years ago, Jodi's husband Brett lost his job in law. But this only served to strengthen Jodi's inner knowing of her purpose. *'We went from six figures to unemployment and food stamps, and it was OK! It was totally fine. It kicked those legs, those wealthy, gold-plated legs, right out from underneath us, and maybe the last of who we were, that last part that we couldn't let go of was finally gone. It made us truly the kind of people that we really, really wanted to be.*

'It left us saying, you know what, we're going to be fine. We're all just going to be fine. We're never going to stop doing what we do. We're never going to stop inviting foster children into our home. We're never going to stop providing. We're never going to stop making good meals. And we'll figure it out. It will be OK. And isn't that what we're supposed to teach our kids? Isn't that what it's all about: just trusting and living on that plane, on that direction that comes right from our heart that says this is where we're supposed to be.

'It's amazing to wake up in the morning and know that your purpose is defined – that you don't need to justify it and that you are simply doing what it is that you're doing because you're supposed to be doing it. It's amazing to put your feet on the ground, and just thank God for another day. OK, here we go, and get up and do it, and know that you're going to make the difference in the life of another person. You don't have to look for it – it's just there.'

Tips for Finding a Purpose

'Pay attention to the signs, pay attention to your gut, to your heart, the outside world, how you are interfacing with it. The transformation will start to begin for sure.' PETER BUFFETT

Having a sense of purpose in life is a great asset because it gives us direction. The question is, though, how do we find it if we don't know what it is?

Peter Buffett offers some simple life advice when he says you should *'pay attention to your gut.'* This is not always easy to do, especially if circumstances force us to focus our immediate attention on other things, but in time, we start to get flashes of ideas and sentiments that point our hearts and minds toward something that is best for us.

John Paul DeJoria says: *'You don't plan it, it just happens. Be open to everything around you and see what direction that takes you in that makes you feel good, without hurting any other human being, and go for it.'*

Birke Baehr thinks it is important for people to *'go out and find their bliss. Follow it and then do it.'* He expands on this: *'If you have fun doing gardening or farming, like me, go for it. Go be a farmer. If you like to make stuff out of wood, go be a carpenter. So one thing: you just need to follow what you like to do,'* he advises.

Scilla Elworthy also believes we should follow our hearts and do what makes us genuinely happy. She encourages us to look for what comes most naturally to us. *'If we can do what really gives us joy,'* she says, *'that is probably something that we find comparatively easy. So the key is to do what comes naturally to us, to shape our life path around what comes easily, and that will be what also makes us able to do it joyfully.'*

She emphasizes the importance of seeking what brings us most joy because we will feel elevated when we do it. *'I think it is really important to search inside for what satisfies us at a very deep level and then there begins to come a kind of glow because we are working from an inner source of power. It is almost like a little power plant inside,'* she says.

Robert E. Quinn also believes in this 'internal power,' maintaining that you will *'never embrace more power than when you embrace your authentic self.'* In his work, Robert has studied exceptional teachers, those who have what he calls 'high value scores.' He explains the process: *'We say to them,"Tell us about your job,"* he says. *'But they don't have a job, they have a calling. They teach because they are called to teach. Their objective is not to 'inform' students, but to transform their lives.'* For these teachers, teaching isn't a job, it's a calling. It is their purpose in life.

Your purpose might be something that you've known since you were a child, something you've always followed. Or maybe you're just finding it now. Peter Buffett says, *'It's not about following some dream because you want to be famous or something. It's about following a dream because it is in you, and you can't help it.'*

Jack Canfield has always followed his instincts in pursuit of his purpose, even when this didn't seem like the most practical thing to do. *'I have been unconsciously aligned with my purpose my entire life because I always followed my heart,'* he explains. *'Whatever my heart was leading me to do, wherever was the greatest sense of joy, curiosity, or lightness, I would go there, and so often at great expense in terms of income or in terms of having to move to follow my next impulse to explore something, to give up a job, a community I was part of. But I was always moving toward my purpose, which I later discovered was to inspire and empower people to live their highest vision in the context of love and joy.'*

How to Tell When You're not Living Your Purpose

If you wake up in the morning and the thought of going to work fills you with dread, that's a sure sign that you aren't living your purpose. Peter Buffett thinks we need to be aware of when our lives are running smoothly, and when they are not. He says we tend to ignore how we feel when life is not working out, and just get on with it.

The key is, he says, not to ignore our feelings at these times. Instead, we need to become aware of what's happening, as he explains: *'So if relationships aren't working out quite right, if you are beating your head against the wall in some job situation, or you have got an upset stomach every morning and you don't know why, those are all things that are telling you that you aren't harmonized with something and you need to look at that.'*

Barbara Marx Hubbard says something similar: *'What I'm finding about life purpose and alignment is that you get an innate sense of joy in doing your life purpose. There's feedback from your own nature. I call it the "compass of joy." So let's say I'm off my purpose and I'm doing things that*

don't work – I feel anxious and stressed. And I have learned
enough; OK, the compass is telling me I'm not on purpose.'

So, it is awareness that starts us on the path to finding
something that is meaningful for us. In the Align Your Purpose
Transformation Program (see p.217) there are a number of
practical tools that can help you to discover your purpose.

The Consequences of Aligning Your Purpose

'I think once you've clarified that position, once you've clarified
your journey, in a way you are almost helping destiny unravel
itself.' JAMES CAAN

Once we find a purpose and align with it, we start to
experience some flow toward it. The current takes us where it
is destined to go, just like the Moon is destined to go around
the Earth. Our purpose energizes us. Sometimes we even
feel a sense of belonging with the idea, and with others who
are also aligned with it who have similar ideas, as they are
also exchanging information with the pattern.

We also become more creative and more productive as we
start to move forward. We sometimes feel what is known
in psychology as 'flow.' Athletes refer to it as being 'in the
zone.' Things seem clearer and easier at these times, like
we've cleaned the dust off the window. When we align with a
pattern, we go with it as it grows, like we're riding the current
of a river. As Gregg Braden says, *'When those patterns fit*
well into the existing patterns, then we feel that there is a
harmony and a flow and an ease.'

Jodi Orton puts it like this: *'I believe that when you truly find your purpose, when you align with who it is that you're here to be, when you are centered on that proverbial axis, that you will thrive.'*

On the other hand, as Gregg also points out, *'When the patterns seem incongruent and they don't fit well with the patterns, we feel like we are going against the flow.'* In other words, if your purpose isn't harmonious with other patterns, then it can feel very difficult to accomplish it.

When we are aligned with a pattern, it feels as if we hardly have to do a thing – and that we are merely participating as our destiny unfurls before us. It can feel like the world is meeting us halfway; that when we put the effort in, successes start lining up for us. We seem to say and do the right things at the right time.

This becomes especially apparent when our purpose is something that serves the needs of a large number of people. We call this a harmonious purpose, in that it is harmonious with the wishes or needs of many others. As we understand reality, these needs will exist as information in our world, and the fractal pattern will have the potential to scale up as we put our efforts into it – as we align with it.

James Caan had this experience when he set up his first major business, a recruitment company called Alexander Mann. His company served the needs of other businesses in that it filled vacant positions more easily, and it also served the needs of those people who were looking for work. In terms of information, the collective business need was information, expressed in various ways, and so the fractal pattern was a potential waiting to happen – to scale up.

It was very much an idea whose time had come and James merely aligned his purpose with it. *'To my amazement it took off almost from day one,'* he says. *'In the first year the business rocketed, in year two it doubled, and in year three it doubled again. I suppose it was one of those right place, right time, right plan, right strategy, right pricing things. I think all the factors came together and it just felt right.'*

Believing in Ourselves

James stresses that belief in ourselves – and in our ideas – at these times is of paramount importance. We can align with a pattern and stay aligned with it by believing in ourselves and in what we are doing. Success then comes more easily, because we are not plagued by doubts.

We don't have to try to 'stay positive' throughout the process either, because we all have 'off' days. One of the strongest messages to come out of our discussions with the change agents featured in this book is that the key to changing their world (and ours) lay more in aligning their purpose by understanding their world (by research and asking questions) than in maintaining a positive mental state. That and an unshakeable belief that they would succeed. This is how we put fuel on our inner fire – by *believing* in it. We exchange much more information that way. With belief comes motivation and action.

Many people in the self-help arena talk about the 'Law of Attraction' – a reference to the general observation that we tend to get what we focus on in life – and many are afraid of having negative thoughts. But when you are aligned with a purpose that is unfolding (the pattern scaling up), the purpose doesn't care so much about your fears or your negative thoughts. If the current is strong enough, and as long as your canoe is in it, you will be carried along.

When we're in this state, we can exceed our own expectations. Scilla Elworthy says, *'When this energy is liberated in a person, they become very creative. They often surprise themselves.'* And with self-belief comes trust, and faith that what we're doing is the right thing for us, as Jack Canfield discovered. He has achieved great personal success in his life by following his heart and trusting that he was doing what he was supposed to be doing. Not only did he achieve success in business, he achieved success inside, too. *'I feel that I have a level of inner peace, a level of contentment, a level of joy, a level of fulfillment that most people I meet don't have,'* he says.

Success Comes in Different Guises

Indeed, success isn't always about personal achievement. Success can mean different things to different people, and wisdom is realizing that it can be the way we lead our lives, the way we treat people, the quality of the relationships we create around us. It can mean being a good parent, or an all-round good person. It can also be getting the learning out of a situation, rather than seeking a result at all costs.

Richard Branson reminds us to trust our gut feeling, our intuition, too. Intuition is, in part, information exchange with a probable or future pattern. Success then opens up for us, even if the circumstances don't look quite right initially. Richard says: *'I think intuition is important and perhaps intuition comes from experience – the experience of falling flat on your face as well as the experience of sometimes succeeding. And if I'm deciding to do something, I don't get accountancy in advance. I do it based on my intuition.'*

Richard's intuition helped him to enter Britain's rail industry. He intuitively aligned with the pattern of what people wanted and made a huge success out of it. *'My gut feeling was if we could bring in brand new trains, if they could be a lot quicker, if we could make sure people's cell phones didn't get cut off all the time, we could give them good access to the Internet, get the staff motivated, then we could make a success of it. So a lot of it is based on common sense and intuition.'*

When we follow our hearts to find our purpose, then, we have the opportunity to experience an increase in the happiness and harmony in our lives. And it doesn't need to be a huge purpose, like changing something in our country, or in the wider world, we can just focus on our own personal world – our families, our jobs, or our social environment.

Peter Buffett touches on this when he says: *'Harmony really can happen in your life, in your relationships, in your physical wellbeing, all those things, if you are centered and following what is your bliss. And that can come in any form. You can be digging a ditch and be thrilled because you have a paycheck you can take home to your family... or you've got wonderful kids. It's not about social status, or amounts of money. It is about harmonizing who you are with the task at hand. And that could be raising kids, being in a great relationship, whatever.'*

Barbara Marx Hubbard explains that having a harmonious purpose gives our lives a sense of direction, a sense of meaning. *'It harmonizes your own energy,'* she says. *'So instead of being depressed, or addicted, or lost, you feel you are going forward.'*

It doesn't matter whether we are impacting on the wider world or just our personal world, then, having a harmonious purpose is merely one that in some way serves the needs or desires of others. And at these times, we are often drawn to those of like mind, just as if we are travelling down the same river current. Our purpose leads us to connect with each other, as Barbara points out: *'You start being aligned with lots of other people, and that feeds back onto your own life purpose.'*

Scilla Elworthy has drawn a similar conclusion from her work with people living in poor or war-torn regions who are determined to make things better for everyone. *'By accessing this internal harmony and energy, it leads us,'* she says. *'Try it and you'll find it. It leads us naturally into contact with other people who have the same feeling of abundance rather than scarcity. The same feeling that there is enough to go round, that we just have to learn to share and to work together.'*

This is because if your purpose is harmonious then others will be aligned with it too. Choice Point is about making a positive difference in the world. Therefore, we'd like to suggest that whatever you do, please ensure that your purpose helps others in a good way.

THINGS TO REMEMBER

1. The first step to aligning your purpose is to define your purpose.

2. Defining your purpose gives you a strong sense of direction in life.

3. Follow your heart to find your purpose.

4. When you are following your purpose, life flows better than when you're not, and you feel better inside.

5. When you live your purpose you benefit from the flow of the pattern it is a part of.

6. Believing in yourself helps you stay aligned.

7. Success can come in different forms. It isn't always about outward achievement.

8. A harmonious purpose is one that serves the needs of others.

CHAPTER 6

DOES MY PURPOSE MAKE A DIFFERENCE?

'In a world that teaches me to achieve, to get honors and recognition, how in the world do I come to discover it is not about me? It is about us.'

ROBERT E. QUINN

We are living in an interesting period in world history and we are now facing a Choice Point regarding the direction we go in next. In these challenging times, we believe that the desire to make the world a better place is one that is supported by millions of people, and that this number is growing. And when our goals are supporting that desire – when they help to make life better for others in some way – those are the goals that will receive the most assistance and be the easiest to attain.

We believe that the most harmonious patterns are those that serve the greater good; those that help the world; and those that help others to expand.

Jack Canfield recalls a conversation he had recently with a friend who *'thinks very, very deeply about these things.'* His friend asked him what he believed was the purpose of the universe. *'I'd never been asked that question before,'* Jack says. *'And so I replied, "I don't know. Let me think about that for a minute." And I kept thinking, what do I know the universe is doing for sure? And I thought, the only thing I know the universe is doing for sure is that it is expanding. We know that from physics.'*

'So eventually I said, "I think the purpose is to expand." My friend agreed with me, saying, "That's right, and anything that supports expansion – the expansions of freedom, the expansion of consciousness, the expansion of abundance, the expansion of love – is going to get supported because it's aligned with what the universe is doing."'

So, if our purpose helps others to expand, it is a harmonious purpose that will be supported by others and, we would say, by the natural pattern of expansion in the universe.

Expanding Goodness

'The most powerful visions are the visions of giving, of expressing love and respect in action.' **BILL DRAYTON**

Of course, there are many activities and disciplines that expand people. Charitable work is one that springs to many minds. But the arts, education, construction, medicine, science, sports, and many other pursuits also help to expand people. And if we can pursue our goals in a way that also supports others along the way, if we treat others with compassion, fairness, and respect, then all the better for all of us because any heartfelt action helps others to expand, and expands us in the process.

Making the world a better place is more than just a psychological desire born out of witnessing human suffering. In fact, we are biologically wired to help each other. It is a biological yearning that evolved out of the natural caretaking behavior of our ancestors. James Caan believes that *'the spirit of giving exists in all of us.'* He adds: *'I think it is love. We just need something to trigger that and bring out that gene in all of us.'*

In these difficult times, making life better for everyone is an inbuilt psychological and biological driver, so we should look at the purpose we choose and the direction we want to go in, and decide whether it serves others in some way. And even if it doesn't, if in the living of that purpose we do so with fairness and respect for others, we not only achieve greater success because we are more supported in our pursuits, but we also get more happiness and inner peace. Bill Drayton advises us that *'The most important guarantee that you will have a rich, happy, healthy life is your figuring out what contribution you can make to the good of all of those around you.'*

When we align ourselves with the desire to make life better for others, or to help others to expand, we align with a harmonious pattern that is growing in the world. The fractal pattern scales up. Every person who demonstrates the innate goodness in him- or herself inspires others, leading to a ripple effect that helps the pattern to grow even bigger.

In her work, Scilla Elworthy has witnessed a growth in the number of initiatives that enable people to help each other. *'In 2001 my research organization mapped the number of initiatives emerging in areas of conflict in the world where local people decided to take peace into their own hands, to build bridges between communities, to go and release child soldiers, to prevent conflict by intercommunal communication, and so on,'* she explains.

'We mapped 400 of these initiatives in war-torn areas like Sudan, Colombia, and Afghanistan and there were approximately 400 reliable, reasonably efficient examples that we came across. If you did the same thing today, you would find at least five times as many examples.'

That's a five-fold increase in the last ten years.

So, we can think of a harmonious pattern as a very large river that is growing all the time because there are lots of smaller rivers running into it. The smaller rivers represent the needs and wishes of lots of people. So, as you align with the river in the pursuit of your goal, you flow (or scale) with it and your goal becomes easier to accomplish because you have the energy of the harmonious river with you. Your goal needs less energy (and fewer resources) to accomplish, and the efforts you make are more fruitful.

A Better Business Model

'All business should be a force for good.' RICHARD BRANSON

What would our world be like if businesses started to align with the maxim above *en masse?* They would still need to survive, of course, and to make a profit, but could this be directed toward building products and services that are of genuine benefit to the world, created without exploiting people or the environment?

John Paul DeJoria says that after he'd experienced some success with his business John Paul Mitchell Systems, he asked himself the following questions: *'Now that we have an abundance – we have more than we ever dreamed about – do we keep building and building and building and buy this for me and this for that? Or do we make the choice and say that success unshared is failure, and make the world a better place for it because we are here?'*

Robert E. Quinn asks us to think about what it would mean for us if we could make things better for everyone. *'The assumptions at the heart of economics, sociology, science, and law say that human beings are self-interested and they are engaged in transactions and exchange. That is the heart of social science,'* he says. *'The question is, when is that not true? What does it mean to create relationships where everyone is getting richer? How in the world do we do that?'*

Gregg Braden adds his thoughts to this viewpoint: *'In business, the idea, based on Darwinian theory, is that it is survival of the fittest and that competition is the model. That's the model that many people embrace. But what if we choose to embrace a business model that is based on cooperation, where we actually give sometimes without receiving in one place, and the receiving comes somewhere else?'*

Gregg has friends who have embraced a cooperative rather than competitive business model, and he says they have been successful with it. *'It worked for my friends, because in embracing this model, they actually embraced a natural pattern that wasn't obvious in the world as we know it today; it is a pattern they were drawn to become a part of, become harmonious with in their hearts. And by allowing that pattern to guide them through their business sense, they were able to succeed where others have not.'*

Jack Canfield offers a similar sentiment. *'We can't live on this planet with the population that's emerging and be competitive, the way we used to be,'* he insists. *'It just won't work. We have to become more cooperative. Now, that might not have been true in the 1800s. There wasn't such a huge population then, but today, when you've got seven roommates in a college dorm room they have got to learn how to get along together. We are all having to do that now. So I think that we need to go from competition to cooperation, and from greed to sharing.'*

The Joy of Giving

'Some people believe that human beings are by nature sinful and have to be redeemed. I don't think that is true at all –

certainly not in my experience. In my experience, human beings are basically generous and have integrity.'
DR. SCILLA ELWORTHY

We experience enormous pleasure when we do things for the common good. Think of how you feel when you do something genuinely kind for another person. It makes you feel good. And that's because kindness is an innate part of us.

Evolution is about survival, but the fittest is not necessarily the strongest or the fastest. The fittest is often the kindest. Our genetic ancestors had to learn to live in small communities to maximize their survival. Forging strong bonds became vital to that survival, and kind behavior was one of the ways those bonds were formed.

The parents in our genetic past had to care for their offspring, too, because those who nurtured their young ensured that they reached reproductive age. And so caretaking genes were 'selected' by nature and passed on to the next generation. Nature also linked caretaking with pleasurable feelings, which increased the likelihood that our ancestors would care for their young, and so the feel-good sensation we get is biologically wired into us.

We feel good when we care for others today because our genetic ancestors cared for each other. If a gene had a goal, its goal would be to survive at all costs, which can be thought of as selfish. But these 'selfish' genes have actually created an organism – a human – that is wired to be kind.

So, when we align our purpose with helping others, not only do we gain creativity and focus, we gain happiness and better health, and of course an inner sense of purpose. Scilla Elworthy finds there are so many personal rewards to be found in helping others: *'It sounds goody goody, but actually it's not. It's actually more fun and more energizing than anything I've ever experienced,'* she says.

And James Caan says he gets great joy and a sense of purpose from his philanthropic work. *'I think it is really funny that when I started on this journey, I never realized the amount of personal gain one really achieves,'* he marvels. *'I had heard the phrase "You receive a lot more satisfaction in giving than you do in receiving," but I didn't know what it meant. It is only when you start that journey that you realize that while you are doing the little you can for people around you, they are actually doing a lot for you.*

'They actually give you a sense of worth,' he adds, *'and the feeling that there is a purpose to your life. It is not just about making money, it is actually what you do with that. And I think this journey for me has been as rewarding, as satisfying for me, as it has been for the people's lives that I have touched.'*

Giving Is Healthy

As you give, you align with a harmonious pattern that is supported by a lot of other people, which in turn gives you a sense of purpose, of destiny. If you are struggling to find a direction in life right now, try giving! If you want something to do, give of yourself in some way in the service of others. You might just find that you have found your calling. You will be aligned with a harmonious purpose and will be nourished by the information carried by it.

Scilla Elworthy describes the joy of giving from the perspective of people who have nothing, and remarks on their amazing warmth and spirit of generosity: *'When you are in a country like Kenya or Uganda, you meet people who really have very, very little, but they will welcome you into their house,'* she says. *'They will give you the last egg that they have – even if their children haven't had an egg for two weeks, they will give it to you. And that just blows me away; that there can be such generosity among people who have nothing. And their lives are warm, they are connected, they are loving. So I don't think it has anything to do with what we possess. I know it sounds trite, but I believe the biggest possession is joy and warmth and a loving family, and to live a life of lovingness.'*

We become expanded when we give, we become more joyful, and our lives become much more fulfilling. As this fractal pattern of giving increases in the world, through more and more people aligning with it, the old pattern of selfishness will come to an end as people start to display more of their natural tendency to kindness. People aligned with the old pattern will begin to feel their world is shrinking and becoming less fulfilling.

Scilla has observed this in her personal world: *'The people I know who are really only interested in their own pleasures and their shares and their dividends, their lives are tending* to close in on them, becoming less and less happy, less and less satisfying, less fulfilling,' she notes. 'They live in gated communities and are rather nervous about who might come and take their big flat-screen TVs. And their lives are getting smaller.'

She also believes that giving can bring health benefits. 'I don't think it has anything to do with possessions. Of course, it helps to have enough money to get about, to eat, to stay warm, but what it's really about is the energy that's available,' she insists. 'Good health and living a generous life, I believe, make our bodies healthier. It is difficult to prove, but nearly all the people I know who are what you might call "in service to the planet" in one way or another live long lives and are very healthy. Not without exception, but that is the norm.'

Scilla then gives us some powerful advice, echoing the words of many great philosophers and wise teachers throughout history: 'So it doesn't really matter how much you have, how much you have control over, or power over. What matters is not what one's holding in, but what one's giving out.'

And she's absolutely right. Modern science shows us that giving is healthy for us. Not only has it been shown to make us happier, it is also good for the heart and, of course, it's good for the soul. Kind behavior is a way to build relationships and strengthen the emotional bonds between people. Emotional bonds produce the hormone oxytocin, which, in addition to its role in reproduction and breastfeeding, helps protect the heart and cardiovascular system from disease.[1,2]

And when giving helps us to form strong relationships with each other, it even helps us to live longer, as modern research also now shows us. Longevity research indicates that having good quality relationships is actually a key factor in living a long life.[3] We are wired for relationships and so when we service them, personally and globally, as we seek to unite in the common good, we live longer, healthier lives, just as if nature is saying to us, *'Yes! This is the way it's supposed to be!'*

The alternative – not to give, not to allow this part of our nature to flower – can wreak havoc on our health, and also on our world. Sometimes, when we go against the flow of our natural tendency, it creates stress in our own minds, which cascades down throughout the body and we end up with stress in our cardiovascular system. And this stresses the whole body.

Being Selfish Takes Effort

'It's not the goal, it's what I call the "come from." Where are you coming from in relationship to that goal?' JACK CANFIELD

Peter Buffett believes that good things come back when we do things for the right reasons, but when we don't, when we are looking for payback in some way, things don't flow as well. He tells us: *'If you put the effort in because it is coming from some deep place of compassion and caring and self-reflection, how you fit in to whatever the situation is, the effort is made in a truthful, honest way, I guarantee good things will come back. But if you are doing it because you really expect something in return, I don't think so. That's not the way to do it as far as I am concerned.'*

Think about it. These are not words that just *sound* like they make sense. They are drawn from the real-life experience of a successful person. We should pay attention to them because many other successful people are saying the same thing: Do stuff kindly, respectfully, and honestly! When we try to create stuff that is not based in something that's positive, creative, making a difference, we can still make it happen, but we have to give it a lot of energy because it is not a harmonious purpose.

Look at it this way: if your goal is selfish, you are providing most of the energy to build it, but when you move your focus away, you no longer provide the energy and so it collapses. But if your goal is harmonious with others, then it is supported, even when you are not there. The overall system carries it and so it keeps going. Selfish goals can feel like we're swimming upstream against a strong current. The moment we stop giving it our attention, the current pulls us right back down again, washing much of our hard work away. People innately want to support what is good.

When we're doing something that's in line with the current, though – something warm, something good for humanity, even something that is good for our loved ones rather than for the entire world – we don't have to give it as much energy because it's in line with the current. And the fruits of our efforts can remain for a long time.

How to Succeed by Doing Good

'I would say if you define success by happiness and fulfillment, then the people that serve others are the most successful.'
PETER BUFFETT

There are positive side effects to aligning your purpose with a harmonious pattern. Jack Canfield draws on his own life experiences to promise you that *'if you make the commitment to align to your purpose, and know that purpose is aligning with the purpose of the universe at that moment in time, you're going to have an extraordinary life – one of great relationships, good health, wonderful joy, fulfillment, contentment, and inner peace. And I believe you deserve that. Everybody on the planet deserves that. That's what we're here for. Don't miss what you are here for!'*

Peter Buffett says we need to have the intention to do what's best for everyone. *'I always come back to intention as being the critical part of success: if we are looking at the world as a place that we are a part of, as opposed to what it can do for us. We need to ask: "How can I serve in the world?"'*

And from a personal point of view he says: *'Yes, I want to be happy and I want to do something that hopefully I enjoy, but it can't be all about me. It has got to be me as connected to the world at large. And I really believe that if you start from that place, unimaginable things can happen in a good way.'*

Peter defines truly successful people as those who serve others. *'There are certainly plenty of what you might call successful people – those who have a lot of things – but they are miserable because they are serving themselves, thinking about themselves,'* he says. *'I guarantee you, the happiest people, the people who feel in their hearts and guts that they are successful, are those who are in service in some way.'*

When we find a way to tailor and align our purposes fully with serving others, this is where the potential for substantial inner and outward success lies. Not only can we experience inner peace and contentment, but there is the potential for us to achieve great things in the world.

Jack Canfield explains the success of the *Chicken Soup* books in these terms. *'The reason they were so successful,'* he says, *'is that we didn't start out to make a lot of money and become millionaires. That wasn't our goal. Our goal was to help transform the world. We wanted to change the world, one story at a time.'*

Committing to a Purpose

'There's a statement that someone uttered once: "At the moment of commitment the universe conspires to help you." And at that point everything starts connecting and the energy starts flowing in such a way that everyone is enlarged, the thinking process is enlarged. Everything increases because you are on that upward spiral.' ROBERT E. QUINN

It is clear that Peter Buffett and Jack Canfield committed themselves wholeheartedly to their purposes. And this is what you must do, too. If you don't fully commit to your purpose, you won't fully align with it.

'Commitment is everything,' Peter stresses. *'Literally, if you don't commit to get out of bed in the morning you are not going to get out of bed. So in the very simplest ways you have to commit to make anything happen, and in the larger sense, when you really commit to something – with the intention that you are moving forward in the world, connected to the world, and understanding you are part of the world – then what you commit to will bring about magical things. All these things happen that never would if you weren't committed.'*

Of course, it isn't always possible to do this. Many of us are in situations where we need to be responsible and stay put. But even then, there can still be opportunities to align with our purpose and commit to it. For instance, imagine you are a lawyer who longs to be a dancer. Aligning yourself with things that support being a dancer is critical, then, but perhaps this is difficult because you have financial commitments. So maybe you can dance on the weekend. If you can earn a living and still do some of what you love, then you are still aligning with it. It is possible to align in less obvious ways, too. You could try being a lawyer for dancers. There are many different ways that we can get ourselves aligned with the world we seek.

Sometimes, having an outlet where we can practice what we love can be enough to bring us happiness. Peter Buffett shares an example of this from his own life: *'When I was in high school and I was playing piano,'* he says, *'it would have been fun to dream of being a pop star and all these things that I saw. I loved the Beatles... I wanna be the Beatles!*

'Well that was not going to happen. But that didn't mean I couldn't fulfil the deeper desire to create music, and to hopefully make people feel something through the music. I've been aligned deeply with something I loved from the time I could walk to the piano and play it.' So, even though Peter couldn't fulfill one particular dream, he could still commit to playing the piano.

Commitment Is Everything

Jack Canfield says that, early in his career, he listened to his gut and acted on it repeatedly, committing himself each time. This commitment eventually led to great success as he explains: *'I took a class in my senior year at Harvard; it was an elective, and it was supposed to be an easy 'A.' It was called Social Relations Tense, and it was like an encounter group, where people would sit around and talk about their feelings. This was totally new to me. I was a macho guy playing rugby and all that, and I discovered my heart and my emotions, and my feelings. It was from that experience that I decided, "I want do more of this, I want to find out about people and understand people."*

'I couldn't get into psychology in graduate school because I had no background training in psychology, though. So someone said, "Well, you can go into education, because you did your major in history and you can teach history.

You can sneak into the other aspects of education over time," which is exactly what I did. I went to the University of Chicago, taught at an inner-city school, joined Jesse Jackson's church, got involved in the civil rights movement.'

So Jack committed to teaching. Then another opportunity came along, and again, Jack chose to commit to it. *'One day, I was in a laundromat and this guy came up to me and said, "Talk to me," he recalls. 'So I put my book down and started talking to him. He invited me to a Living Philosopher series that was taking place in northern Chicago. One of the presenters there – the director of the National Centre for the Exploration of Human Potential – claimed we are only using 10% of our brains, and I thought, "Wow, what's the other 90% doing?"*

'I went up to him afterwards and told him I wanted to do what he was doing, and asked how I could find out more. He told me there was a foundation in Chicago exploring it all, so I went there and started taking the workshops they were running. In the first year I did something like 27 workshops. Every weekend, Christmas, New Year's, I was training, learning more about the self, and about the body, and about emotions, and about consciousness, and that was a major shifting point in my life.'

Jack made a real commitment by acting on the opportunities he was given and then putting in many hours of learning through attending all those workshops. The physical shift came in his life because he committed fully to his heart's desire.

THINGS TO REMEMBER

---

1. A harmonious purpose helps other people to expand.

2. The amount of goodness and helping in the world is increasing.

3. Businesses would benefit us more if they were based on cooperation rather than competition.

4. We are genetically wired to be kind and to help each other.

5. Helping others is healthy and helps us live longer.

6. Pursuing goals takes more effort when we're being selfish.

7. Committing to a purpose is essential.

What You've Learned So Far

In Part 1, we revealed that the world is fractal based and that it is important to understand the patterns in your life. We showed you that you can do this by research and asking questions, and that as you come to understand your world, you can predict which patterns are likely to be harmonious in the future.

In Part 2, we explained that you can think of reality in terms of information and energy and that the entire universe, including you, is interconnected, or *entangled*. You learned that to align with a pattern, you need to exchange information with it, and that you can do this with your thoughts, emotions, beliefs, and actions.

We also explained that you need to define your purpose, so you have direction in your life, and that the most harmonious purposes are those that support the needs and desires of humanity.

In the next part of the book, we look at commitment more fully, because if you want to change the world, you need to commit to *being* the change.

PART 3
BE THE CHANGE

CHAPTER 7
HOW TO BE THE CHANGE

'We change the world by changing ourselves.'
ROBERT E. QUINN

Just as in the 'butterfly effect' – when a butterfly flapping its wings in one part of the world can have consequences for the weather somewhere else on the planet – a small change to the source of a fractal can produce quite large changes in the pattern. From our perspective, this means that as we change ourselves, we change the world around us because the patterns in the world reflect our hearts and minds. The bigger the internal change we make, the bigger the change we see.

And if we change by moving ourselves into alignment with patterns that are harmonious with large numbers of people, we become entangled with those patterns and exchange information and energy with them. And in turn, the patterns support us, helping us to achieve what we want in life. Making inner changes to our ideas, values, hopes, dreams, and actions can lead to changes in our social, political, and economic landscapes, too. As we change ourselves, we change our world.

Here's a way to understand how this simple mechanism works. Imagine that each person has a mental and emotional climate that is represented by a colored cloud above his or her head. One person's clouds mix and merge with other people's clouds as they exchange information with them. So, we might observe areas with the same cloud color as people with a similar mindset come together. We might even find that households, towns, cities, and even nations have the same overall tone to their clouds, as many people are aligned with the same patterns.

If we could look at this picture from above, we might see patterns of colors swirling and moving as we constantly exchange information with each other and with reality. Now imagine that people begin to change themselves so much that the color of their cloud changes, too. We're all exchanging information, so this color might then begin to filter into neighboring people's clouds, tinting them too. And as the clouds represent those people's mental and emotional climates, so they begin to change too, creating a ripple effect.

So perhaps in this way, as we *become* the changes we want to see in the world, we actually can change the world. As Dr. Rainer Viehweger points out: *'We live in a fractal universe, which means we are all universes, only smaller. By changing the universe inside of us, we will change the whole universe.'*

Change is Contagious

'As you change yourself, you will become open to and aware of new insights and new ideas.' **ROBERT E. QUINN**

As we change our thinking and behavior, then, we exchange different information with reality. We resonate with different patterns around us. And as these patterns (as well as ourselves) exchange information with other people, we might find that people around us become inspired, especially if what we are doing is heartfelt, and something that makes a positive difference. In a sense, we become contagious.[1] Indeed, social network research at Harvard University and other institutions in the US has shown that kindness, happiness, depression, obesity, alcohol consumption, smoking, and even divorce are contagious. A change in any one person seems to have a ripple effect through our social networks.

But it is not enough just to change our minds. We need to go beyond that. We need to make a *lasting* change, otherwise it will be very easy for us to slip back into our old mindset again, or for changes to revert to the previous patterns. Making complete changes within ourselves, and in our lives, ensures that a change in our reality is more permanent, as Gregg Braden explains: *'One of the fundamental principles that comes to light again and again is that when we choose to change something in our lives – the healing of our bodies or the physical reality around us – it is not enough to simply think about the change or wish or hope for the change,'* he says.

'To the best of our ability, we must become in our lives the very things that we choose to experience in the world. We must become the healing, we must become the cooperation, we must become the peace, and live that principle every moment of every day in our lives, before we can actually experience it in our world.'

But is it really possible to change anything? Since patterns and cycles give us a sense of destiny, do we have free will to change things, especially if the patterns that surround us guide our behavior?

Destiny vs Free Will

'I think there are a number of different factors and forces that come together to craft or create the opportunity for destiny to be played out. And I think we play a hand in it.' JAMES CAAN

We believe that there is interplay between destiny and free will. As we've learned, patterns and cycles surround us and influence our lives. When we are carried by a pattern we experience what feels like destiny as we, often unknowingly, move toward the pattern's destination – as we constantly exchange information with it.

So part of free will is in how much we understand this so that we can make different choices where we want to.

When we fully understand the processes of cycles and information exchange, we get the sense that we are able to make choices, rather than being controlled by the natural patterns that permeate our lives. We feel we have a degree of control, rather than being blown around like a leaf in the wind.

As we become wiser and our understanding of our world increases, we'd expect to have more free will, but actually we are then using free will to surrender to destiny in the patterns we purposefully align with. With this wisdom and understanding, we begin to align with and surrender to patterns and cycles – as we align our purpose, we get carried by the wind. Free will, then, is in continuing to make the right choices so we stay aligned.

The more we understand our world, the more destiny can help us, because patterns have an end point that they can carry us toward, just as a current on a river has a destination. Of course, even though we are surrendering to the 'destiny-ation' of a current (pattern), we are still using free will to *choose* that current. In this way there is a constant interplay, at least in our own minds, between destiny and free will. So a deeper question we might then ask ourselves is: are we really exercising free will in life or just being free with the dance?

Whether it is destiny or free will that is dominant, though, is a debate that has existed forever. Alison Pothier sums up the typical dilemma most of us have when she asks: *'Is this fate and destiny and are you just part of it? How much control have we got over all of this?'*

Can We Change Our Course?

Many people side in favor of destiny, especially when they look at some of the problems in the world. They wonder whether a disastrous outcome is inevitable, if it is predestined, and whether we can change the direction we seem to be heading in. They wonder whether this is the way things are supposed to be and think, "What's the point in being a positive change if it doesn't actually matter what we do because we're headed for disaster anyway?"

When some people think of destiny, they imagine we're born for a purpose and that our lives are mapped out for us. Perhaps this is true. We have no way of knowing for sure. Perhaps human consciousness preexists in some form (a larger or higher spiritual form) before we are born, as some spiritual and wisdom traditions teach. They also teach that we remain attached to this form and sometimes, in certain transcendent states, we tap into and feel this larger part of ourselves.

If this is true, then, perhaps we do have a hand in deciding the conditions we are born into, even though, once we are born, we retain no memory of it. In these terms, if we are born on purpose, then much of the direction of our lives is mapped out, especially as we live in a world of patterns and cycles because, as we have explored, these cycles may force social and economic events upon us.

Our higher self would know what was coming if it chooses the conditions we are born into, but the key is that, despite the natural cycles that come around in our individual and collective lives, we have a *choice* in how we react to them, as we learned in the first part of the book, and we can also choose certain patterns to align with, as we learned in the second part.

There is a line of reasoning on this subject that can be described metaphorically. Imagine your life as a train and the track, which represents the patterns and cycles of which your life is a part, has a particular destination. Perhaps you were born on that track, but there are many other tracks, led by different patterns, each with their own destination. By making different choices in life, you can exchange information with different patterns, and therefore jump to a different track with a *different* destination.

This might be as you act upon an idea, a hope or a dream, or a purpose that you feel is yours. And so your choice, which is your free will, takes you toward a new destination, determined by the track that you are now on – in other words, the pattern you are now aligned with.

Changing Tracks

Physician and author Larry Dossey gives an excellent example of changing tracks. He describes how a young mother had what seemed like a terrible nightmare about her baby. In the dream she saw a chandelier fall on top of the baby as it lay sleeping in its cot. She also saw that the weather was stormy and that the time on the clock was 4:30am. She was startled awake.

The dream felt so real that the woman woke her husband and together they went to check on the baby – all was well. By then, it was after midnight and the weather was calm. The couple returned to their bed but the woman just didn't feel right. She couldn't settle. The dream felt too real to her. So after a while she got up and brought the baby back to bed with her. Later that night, the couple were woken by a loud crash. They rushed through to the baby's room, and saw that the chandelier had fallen on top of the cot. The weather had turned stormy, and the woman noticed that the time on the clock was 4:30am – exactly as she had dreamed.

We would say that the baby being killed by the falling chandelier existed as a real probability – a real track – something that was likely to occur should a different choice not be made. But the woman *did* make a choice and so she changed to a different track, one where her baby was safe. We would say that she used free will to overrule the unfolding pattern she was aligned with at the time.

Larry Dossey interprets the event this way: *'I see the future as probabilistic. I think what people see in premonitions is the most probable or likely outcome. But that doesn't mean it is written in stone and is unchangeable.'*

He proposes the theory that the future is changeable, and that there are multiple possible outcomes. In at least one interpretation of quantum mechanics, all possible futures (and pasts) are thought to exist and the one we experience is the one we choose. In these terms, when a person has a premonition, they might be sensing what the most likely outcome will be if they stay on the current track. And premonitions like these give us opportunities to make changes to the direction we are heading in.

As Larry explains: *'The chandelier had certainly fallen and wrecked the bed, but it had not harmed the baby because the mother took action in the present to change the future and save the life of her child.'*

We don't need a premonition though, to see that the world is currently facing a great number of crises. Left unchecked, the most likely outcome for us all could well be more wars, more poverty, more starvation, and more economic collapse. The question is – is this what you choose?

We are faced with a Choice Point right now. The power to change the world lies in each and every one of us. If we want to change the world, we need to *be* the change.

So how do we do that?

Matching

'The vast majority of the time, when people are frustrated in trying to bring change, it is because they've behaved in a way that prevents change from happening.' ROBERT E. QUINN

Matching is the concept of like attracting like. Similar pieces of information match (or resonate) with each other and so become connected, just like a tuning fork will inspire the same sound in another tuning fork, becoming connected to it by the same sound. What we are thinking and, more importantly, what we are *being* colors the information that we give out, or transmit, and so we match with similar information.

We are like radios in that we broadcast a signal that carries the information of what we are thinking and how we are behaving. Our signal matches with the signal of a station and we become tuned to that station. It's as if our thinking and our way of being turns the dial.

We are matching all the time, only most of us don't realize what we are matching to. In simple terms, if a person has a scattered and chaotic mind, they will match with other things that are scattered and chaotic. Their living space will probably be cluttered and messy and events and circumstances in their life will seem disordered and random.

In this way, many of us tend to get the things in life that we give the most attention to, because these things *match* with us. This is great if we're focusing on positive things, but too often we dwell on stuff we don't really want to have in our lives. The more we dwell on it, the more we match with it because that's where our focus is, and so the longer it stays with us.

On the positive side, we can use matching to align ourselves fully with what we'd like to be, or to accomplish. But how do we do that? It's OK to have a focus in our minds but, as Gregg Braden said earlier, that isn't always enough. To fully match with what we want, we need to live it and breathe it.

Let's say you want to become an actor. You'll have to start behaving like an actor – mimicking people, speaking in different accents, taking on another persona. Eventually, you may even apply for acting roles. Going further, in order to match more completely, you might even make your own film and give yourself a starring role in it. In doing all this, you'll become a total match for acting. Matching is a practical way of getting into alignment with something!

On the other hand, if you are matching with the vibe of a librarian, there is much less chance you'll land a part in a movie. You might still get a few roles, because of your mental goal, but they are unlikely to be of any great significance because you are not fully matching in your behavior. It's as if you are focusing your *mind* on something that is out to your left but focusing your *body* (your actions) to the center. So what you get is halfway in between the two.

Being Clear About What We Match To

You also need to be quite certain about *what* your goal is. Having just a vague idea of what you want is of little use because you won't know how to fully match to it and could end up groping around in the dark. If you want to write, for example, you need to think about the *kind* of material you want to write: is it books, poetry, screenplays, a blog? What we get back from the world is only as good as the information we put out, because it is what we match to.

With this simple idea, you can become the director of the film of your own life. What you experience is a consequence of what you match to. This idea is highly empowering because you don't have to feel helpless, floating in a world of circumstances beyond your control. And, as you learned earlier, if you match with harmonious patterns, all the better for you.

To create real, positive change with your goal, though, you'll need to give it your complete focus. You'll need to *act* on it. Action is highly important, says James Caan. *'The reality is, the idea only represents 5% of the journey, of making it happen. 95% of it is execution. And to me, execution is where the strength and the journey of success lies, not in the idea.'* And John Paul DeJoria urges us to *'Do something about it! Don't be lazy! Take action!'*

Matching gives us the sense that we can succeed, because we are just following a simple process of deciding what we want and then matching with it. We can trust that beneficial things will be happening in the background, whether we are aware of them or not, because what we match to is much bigger than we are, just as the pattern of acting extends much further than a person's own life. We can think of what we match to as like a wave at the seashore. The wave is much wider than the part that washes over our feet – it carries to the shore much more than the little bit we experience – but as we are matching to the wave (exchanging information with it), we attract some of the wave's experiences to us.

Other people are also aligned with the patterns we match to. So people connected with the information around that idea will be attracted to us and us to them, in the sense that like attracts like, since we are all exchanging information. We are all part of the wave, or the pattern.

Matching with Higher Principles

So, what if we want to really impact the world in a positive way? As we've learned, thinking about it isn't enough and neither is just talking the talk. We can learn a lot from inspirational figures in our recent history, such as Gandhi, Martin Luther King, and Nelson Mandela. They show us that if we want to create big changes we need to fully *become* what we stand for – to live and breathe what we speak about.

Scilla Elworthy talks about Nelson Mandela's attitude during the 27 years he spent in prison. He and his fellow inmates were badly treated by some of the guards, but she says they *'learned to constantly turn this treatment around and treat their tormentors with generosity, respect, and patience. And Mandela was also training himself and his fellow prisoners to an Olympic standard of wisdom, compassion, and tolerance, which became invaluable in preventing civil war when he came out.'*

Mandela and his fellow prisoners stuck to their principles. The transformation that he – and many other inspirational change agents – stood for was the common good: a harmonious pattern. As we know, the more people who want a particular change, the more harmonious it will be and in general, a harmonious change will often come from your heart and not your head.

Robert E. Quinn says that *'everybody can make a positive difference.'* Which means paying attention to what's in our hearts and minds, to how we treat people, to our personal values and motivations, and to our behavior. We need to look within ourselves with a high degree of honesty to do this. So the first step in *being* the change is to *look within.*

Look Within

'You must know who you are and you must embrace who you are in order to then go beyond it.' **ALISON POTHIER**

Looking within requires us to be honest with ourselves and identify thinking and behavior (our patterns) that may be blocking us from moving in the direction we want to go. For example: are we *hoping* for change on the one hand, but not really *being* it on the other?

The first step is to accept that the world *inside* is related to the world *outside;* that our own thinking has a hand in creating many of the circumstances in our lives. This is an empowering idea because it means that if we create some of the bad stuff, we can create something else, too.

But often when we look within ourselves we don't like what we see. Many reject that there can be any association at all between our experiences in life and the contents of our minds, but that doesn't help us to change. It is only when we accept this inner-outer connection that we can change things in our lives.

The second step, Alison Pothier says, is understanding that if it is inside of us, then we are in control of it, which *'puts us in*

an empowered place for the first time and we think, alright,
I will listen for a minute if I might be able to change it.'

And from this empowered place we are able to change, as
Alison states: *'The third step is to say, OK, great, see what is*
outside of you that you want changed. Be it. Be the change
you want to see. Go inside, have a look at what it is that
is creating the world out there. Work with it. Befriend it
somehow. Go there. And when you come out the other side,
arrive differently in the world to make the impact in the
world that you saw needed to be changed. Just realize you
didn't have to go anywhere to do that. You just had to delve
inside.'

So before we can *be* a change, we need to understand
and accept that what we see in our own personal world is
very often a projection of our inner world, just as we have
suggested that patterns and cycles throughout the universe
are projections of patterns and cycles on the inside of atoms.

The way to change our lives or change the world is first
to *look within* to find what we need to change and then *be*
the change.

Arriving differently in the world

Alison Pothier gives us a practical example of this process.
'Say I am running a belief system that says I am too small
to matter. So in the outside world I get that affirmed back
to me over and over again,' she begins. If we hold this type
of belief, we may experience a life in which we are treated as

insignificant, our opinions considered unimportant. We may be consistently overlooked for promotion at work, too. Painful as it can be, we need to acknowledge that we are seeing this reality in our lives because of the belief we hold inside that it is true.

But from this space of honesty and acceptance, we can be empowered to change, as Alison explains: *'So, I decide on a given day to go in to work and say, even though I think or feel that I am too small to matter, and that really hurts, I completely and totally trust and believe that I do matter; that something I am here to contribute won't get done.'*

The words 'even though... I completely and totally trust and believe...' are a gentle way for us to change without beating ourselves up for having had a different idea about ourselves. *'I come and make that change in me,'* Alison continues. *'So I am now in a new energy and a new belief system. And I arrive in the world with the belief system that I can make an impact. I am no longer too small to matter. I actually matter. So I start making a difference because of the fact that I've decided to accept my vulnerability and walk with it hand in hand.'*

So, changes in our outer lives come because of changes in our inner lives.

Of course, it's not always easy to see what's inside. It can be quite an emotional experience. Alison has had a lot of painful experiences in her professional and personal life. She experienced jealousy at work, and her husband had an affair. She had to look within herself to see whether her own thoughts and behavior were somehow being reflected in these experiences. *'For instance, to see career jealousy created outside of me, I needed to find where I was creating career jealousy inside of me,'* she explains. *'I suppose I would have had to look at whether or not I wanted other people's jobs or what I would do to position for other people's jobs.'* In other words, she had the experience of people making covert moves for her job in the company she worked for, so she had to consider that she might also be *wanting* other people's jobs and making moves toward them.

And her husband's betrayal also encouraged her to look within. *'To have a fear of affairs occurring outside of me, I had to find out where I had affairs inside of me,'* she says. Although Alison didn't have an affair herself, her husband's behavior involved lying to get what he wanted, so Alison had to consider where she might lie in her life to get what she wants. In other words, her husband's behavior could have been part of a 'lying' pattern. *'What I had to learn is that in me is a cheater. In me is someone who could lie consistently in order to have my cake and eat it too,'* she says.

Of course, it's not exactly the same thing but it's the same *kind* of thing. Having her husband cheat wasn't a reflection of her personally having an affair, but the behavior of lying to 'have her cake and eat it too' was a reflection of that *capability* in her. *'So every single thing that was falling to pieces around me was a belief system which needed to be rebuilt within me, and that began the transformation process,*' Alison says. And this is where real change began for her.

Addressing the Hypocrite Inside

'It's about becoming more and more conscious – conscious of myself and what's going on around me.' **ROBERT E. QUINN**

How many times have you accused someone of a failing in their behavior, only to have them point the finger right back at you? This could even be something as trivial as untidiness around the house. Most of the time we refute the other person's claim, but in this book we are encouraging you to say: 'OK, where *is* that true for me?' It is only through being honest about what is going on in our minds that we can make the necessary breakthroughs in being the changes we want to see.

'You can't sit there and say, "I want peace in the world" if you are constantly arguing with your children, your wife, your neighbors, your boss, and so on,' Jack Canfield declares. *'Normally, when we're arguing out here, it's because we are arguing with some part of our self that we haven't fully embraced,'* he adds.

Gregg Braden offers his view on the subject. *'We find ourselves in situations that we would like to change, situations that are uncomfortable for us,'* he says. *'And I think part of the maturity that comes from understanding our relationship to the matrix is the honesty with which we look at ourselves and ask the question, "What is it about myself that I am seeing in the world around me that I would like to change?" Is it something that I don't like in the world, that I don't like in my family, or in my workplace? How does that relate to something that I am, or that I claim in my personal life?'*

Of course, with painful events it is certainly not easy to consider that your personal beliefs could have had a hand in creating them. Many times they don't, because patterns and cycles bestow conditions upon us, but there are more occasions than many of us would care to accept when they do. Our beliefs affect our behavior and so there are times when we create for ourselves situations that confirm those beliefs.

It can be especially painful to consider that some of the negative behavior we see in others is actually in *us* too. Commonly, what we dislike or judge in others is also part of who we are. When seeing someone display anger, for instance, we might not want to accept that we also feel anger about things, especially if we have a spiritual practice that encourages us to work on inner peace.

A Hall of Mirrors

What we need to address is often obvious, but there are many times when it is less so, and requires us to look a little deeper. And this can feel like being in a hall of mirrors and seeing deeper and deeper versions of yourself, as Gregg Braden explains: *'Sometimes we might find people that are truly angry or judgmental and we ask ourselves: are they mirroring my anger and my judgment? And sometimes they might be. But if the answer is no, if we can honestly say, I am not the anger and the judgment that I am seeing around me, then it invites us to look at the next level of the mirror.*

'*So, if people aren't mirroring what we are, then it is very possible they mirror the things that we judge in ourselves. And maybe those angry, judgmental people are showing us our judgment and the little things that we actually judge in ourselves. This is a little more subtle way of looking at mirrors.*'

Seeing anger and judgment doesn't necessarily mean that we are being angry and judgmental toward others. If we can honestly say this isn't the case, and examine ourselves a little more deeply, we might discover that the anger and judgment we see outside of us is actually *mirroring* the anger and judgment we feel toward ourselves. In this way, what is *inside* of us is still experienced *outside* of us. You might consider it as a scaled-up fractal pattern of the judgment.

If we see conflict around us – in our personal world of family, social, and work environments – or if conflict in the world occupies our attention, it might be mirroring a conflict in *how* we are living our lives compared to how we *want* to live our lives, or even how we *think* we should live our lives. For some, this might be a conflict around money; for others it might be with their sexuality or even a conflict between their hearts and minds. If someone has hurt or offended you, your heart naturally wants to forgive. This is both a spiritual and a biological yearning. But your mind usually wants some form of revenge.

So, now there is a conflict between your heart and your mind, and the wars that you see around you faithfully reflect back to you this struggle within yourself.

Peace: As Within, So Without

'What is the world showing me about myself?' **GREGG BRADEN**

Let's say your thoughts are preoccupied with the wars and conflicts in the world. You can ask yourself: 'Where is the war inside of me?' We'd hazard a guess that most people, if they are honest with themselves, can find such a war inside them. And if this is true for you, then you are at a personal Choice Point.

Jack Canfield has a neat way of summing this theory up: *'We always think the world would be better if only those people out there would change, and the fact is the change has to start within ourselves,'* he says. *'There will continue to be conflict in the outer world as long as there is conflict inside the individual.*

'There's a great Chinese saying,' he adds, *'that goes something like this: "When there is peace in the individual*

there will be peace in the house, there will be peace in the community. And when there is peace in the community there will be peace in the nation. When there is peace in the nation there will be peace in the world."'

Jack encourages us to think of our own lives in these terms, and asks us: *'If we can't even get along in our own country with our neighbors, how do we think we're going to have the Palestinians and the Israelis solve their problems?'*

The world reflects our own selves back to us, then. And so to change what we see in the world, the place to start can only be inside ourselves, in our own hearts and minds. Jack serves up a bowl of advice based on his own personal experiences in life. *'We have to learn how to meditate and do other spiritual practices to create inner peace within us,'* he urges. *'So we come to people all inclusive, and accepting and loving, and not creating conflict with them. And that grows out like dropping a stone into a pond, those ripples expand outward.'*

When you truly make peace within yourself, don't be at all surprised if what you see in your world begins to change. We are suggesting that it is not only that the outside reflects back to us the world on the inside, but that much of the time, the inside actually *causes* the outside, at least in our personal lives, and this is why changing ourselves can have such a powerful impact.

'For' Rather Than 'Against'

Many people today are deeply passionate about having peace in our world. Many lead by example in their own households; others are activists with peace in their hearts and minds. But some unleash anger and aggression in their quest for peace. Their goal might be powered by a passionate belief in the type of world they wish to inhabit, but they are matching with anger and aggression and so they create ripples of anger, aggression, and even violence as well ones of peace.

Their actions may produce peace in the end, but not without conflict during the process. *'Being angry about something that we don't like in our world is probably not going to help change what we don't like,'* Gregg Braden warns. *'And it may actually contribute to the very conditions we would most like to shift.*

'Angrily protesting war for example, with thousands of other people who are angrily protesting war, serves the purpose of bringing attention to that cause, but it may also add fuel into the field, into the fractal patterns of experience, the very anger that is the basis for the war that we would like to end.'

It is our belief that we should move away from ideas like, 'the war against... ' and instead embrace the idea of 'in support of.' Fighting against something, like war, doesn't do as much good as we would hope it would. We align with the 'fight' pattern instead of the 'peace' or 'reconciliation' one. We have to become warlike to fight against war, and so we match with, or become, the very thing we oppose. Of course, we want to transform the ills of the world, but how we go about it is important. The way we sometimes go about things isn't the most harmonious or the way of least energy. To stop war, choose peace. As Archbishop Desmond Tutu advises us, we need to choose *'the path of forgiveness instead of revenge, the path of reconciliation instead of retribution.'*

So, the key to being the change is to look within to find our internal beliefs and conflicts, and then to actually, practically, be the change we need to be, so that what is now inside of us gets firmly projected onto the outside.

Returning to Our True Selves

Jack Canfield says that looking within allows us to rediscover ourselves and return to the essence of who we really are, removing the layers of emotional scarring that many of us have that obscure our true majesty. He offers a simple metaphor to help us understand this. Some time ago, during a trip to Thailand, he visited the temple of the Golden Buddha. The Buddha is the largest solid gold object on the planet, but 50 years ago, no one realized that it was gold.

'We were looking at this Buddha,' Jack explains, *'and off to the side there was this piece of clay in a frame that said in 1957, the Thais didn't know there was such a thing as a Golden Buddha. They had a clay Buddha, which they were moving with a crane when a crack went down through it. They covered it because it was starting to rain. When they came back out at night and shone a flashlight in it to see*

if it was staying dry, something reflected back from inside. "Clay doesn't reflect light, so there must be something else in there," they said. And sure enough, inside the clay was a Golden Buddha.

'Their best theory is that about 300 years earlier, the Burmese were attacking Thailand. The monks knew the attack was coming, so they covered the Buddha up with clay to make it look like it was worthless so the Burmese wouldn't steal it and melt it down. They think all the monks were killed and that the secret died with them. And so this was discovered many, many years later.'

Jack reads this as a symbol of what we need to do in our lives. *'I love the word "discovered," because it means to take the cover off something that is already there,'* he explains. *'So I think people would naturally be aligned with their purpose if they hadn't had all of this training in school, and religious training, and parental training, and wounds and hurts and traumas and so forth, that put this layer of clay over the golden essence of who they really are.'*

He says that our work is to *'get rid of the clay.... to get rid of the fears, to get rid of the emotional scarring and wounding that's occurred throughout our lives so that we can get back to the essence of who we are and not be run by the fears of limiting beliefs.'*

Because when we do this, we can make some great transformations in our lives.

THINGS TO REMEMBER

---

1. Changing ourselves ensures that a change is a lasting one.

2. We need to be a match for what we want.

3. There is an interplay between destiny and free will.

4. We can choose how we act within natural cycles and choose to align with specific patterns.

5. The outer world reflects the inner world.

6. If we look within, we can discover our inner world.

7. If we want to see peace in the world, we need to be peaceful.

8. If we look inside and deal with any emotional wounds, we can discover our true selves.

CHAPTER 8
MAKING THE CHANGES

*'In order to truly transform, from the depths of
drug addiction and a life of crime, I had to look
deep within myself and face my own darkness. I had
to love myself for what I was, and this helped me
to turn that darkness into light.'*

BRETT MORAN

British addiction specialist and health coach Brett Moran is
a living example of how looking inside ourselves, and then
matching with something different, can lead to profound
changes. In his early 20s, Brett was severely addicted to crack
cocaine, and used cannabis and alcohol to pass out. He was
also living a life of crime, and spent time in prison. He reached
the depths of despair, and even contemplated suicide.

One day in the prison library, though, his life began to change.
He'd arranged to meet a fellow inmate there in order to buy
some heroin from him. The prison guards were watching,
so Brett pretended to be looking at the books. He pulled
one out at random. The book was on meditation and it was

called, *Moment by Moment: Art and Practice of Mindfulness*. When Brett glanced at the back cover, the words caught his attention and immediately had a profound effect on him.

'As I was reading the back of the book, I became mindful in that moment, and I started to read; it was saying you can become aware of your thinking,' Brett recalls. *'And at that moment, being in prison, my thinking was constantly negative. "I wish I didn't do this or I should have said that" – all that sort of stuff was going over and over. And I thought, if this book can really shut my mind up and give me a moment of peace, or awareness or clarity, then it's worth its weight in gold.'*

Brett borrowed the book from the library, which was something he had never done before, and from that moment on, he started to look inside himself a little, becoming aware of his self-destructive thoughts. That night, he said a prayer in his cell – again something that he was definitely not accustomed to doing.

He explains what happened next: *'I sort of made a vow to myself and I just said, if the book is in any way insightful or truthful, or if there was anything out there such as Buddha or God or anything, then I would make a conscious promise to myself to change, to really try to put something different into the world, to really become different. I opened my eyes and I was still in that same prison cell, but I just felt something inside. I closed my eyes, fell asleep.'*

From that day on, Brett says, the prison sentence just didn't seem as bad. *'It seemed as if I was just going through it;*

I was just experiencing the moment. I carried on reading the book, and something just sank deep, deep inside me that it was true, it was real. And it was nothing special, nothing outside of the box, it was inside, everything inside me. I'd become aware of the thoughts that I was generating. I'd become aware of the feelings that I was in conflict with.'

Life Is a Journey

The experience began a gradual process of deep change in Brett's mind. Life didn't completely change for him from that moment on; he still had many ups and down to go through. *'One day I'd be praying in Thailand, the next day I'd be in a bar completely out of my face, taking drugs, living that yin and yang life again,'* he admits. But the experience did begin a completely new journey for him.

'I think I had a series of events from that day forward,' he says. *'I had different teachers come into my life. I had prison sentences, I had more drugs to take, but then I had spiritual moments, like in Thailand; I said another prayer, had my daughter, Ella Louise. I can't say there was one time when I just thought, "That's it, I'm giving up drugs," but these positive things made me open my eyes; the more often they happened, the more they reinforced the idea that maybe there was a different path for me, another possibility. Maybe there is a new life out there for me to enjoy, to embrace.'*

These experiences taught Brett that *'life is a journey and not a destination.'* And from this mindset he was gradually able to shift his view enough to start seeing his world in a different way. He says, *'I realized I had to go through the good and the bad events in my life. I started to see the bad events in a positive kind of way, too, realizing they were mistakes and lessons to allow me to grow, to evolve more. And obviously I noticed the lighter and more positive events in my life: the feel-good factor, the great things. And it wasn't two weeks and then I was completely cured, sitting on a mountain meditating. It was a whole journey, a long journey until this day. I'm forever learning.'*

The power of looking inside had initiated a great transformation and Brett was beginning to match with a new pattern. After his release from his second prison sentence, he decided that he had to make some real changes to his life and get away from drugs once and for all. But for that to happen, he would have to physically remove himself from the only place he had ever known as home. He would have to move away from his old life to a brand new place where he would meet different people. He would have to make an even stronger commitment to change.

In the past, by living in the same place and with the same people, Brett had always been drawn back into the world of drugs, even when he'd wanted to quit. If he moved, he would be giving himself the chance to be different. But that world was all he knew. It was a life he shared with the only friends he had ever had, the only real sense of connection he had with anything. *'It was probably one of the hardest things, apart from giving up drugs,'* Brett confesses. *'Because moving away from them felt like I was losing something else, more than just the drugs and the money. I was losing that attachment, that connection that I was trying to create constantly. It was very difficult.'*

But he knew that deep change in his life would require deep personal change and that he had to fully commit to it. *'I moved to a little village about seven miles from the nearest town; it felt like I was living in the woods, in the sticks. I completely dropped all my friends, dropped all the drugs, dropped all the crime. Didn't have a car or even a cell phone. To me, it was like a detox from my friends, a detox in my mind, and it was somewhere I could rebuild my life, rebuild positive beliefs for myself.'*

A New Vision

Brett began to build a new life for himself: *'I went to college, did an introduction to counselling, and while I was there I saw a sign on the wall asking for volunteers for a drug and alcohol drop-in centre,'* he says. He was already beginning to match with helping others, so he applied for and got that volunteer position, working long hours between his college course, solidifying his personal changes. *'It was quite tough – and exhausting,'* he says, *'but it felt brilliant, it felt like it was a different path that I was choosing. I felt like that was where I should be.'*

And from there, Brett's purpose became clearer. He began to define it. *'When I was connecting with these homeless people, these addicts, I could see in them what I couldn't see in myself. I started to find something in myself and when I looked at them, they were just the same as me. They were just human beings: that beauty was inside them. And when I saw that in them, I felt that was my purpose, to be able to help them to see that inside themselves; let them find that light in them, and then whatever they wanted to do with that, hopefully become happy and enjoy life.'*

Brett was eventually taken on by the charity as a paid employee, but he says that he *'didn't do it for the money, or for the career. I did it because I found the light. It sounds a bit over-the-top, but I felt like I'd found something inside me that was my gift. My gift was to connect with others, and help them find their gift. And it just felt so normal to be able to connect with people.'*

Brett had now found his purpose, and it was aligned with something much bigger than himself. His purpose served others, and he was a complete match for it. The change started *inside* him, and then he moved completely into alignment with what he wanted and fully *became* the change. He lived it and breathed it, and this is why his life completely changed. It wasn't just a change in his thinking, or a change in his desire, he actually *lived* the change and this is why it became permanent.

Brett offers some advice to people who are considering taking a leap of faith in their pursuit of a new life: *'I know sometimes it is hard to jump, but once you do it, it becomes a lot easier, and not so daunting. It is not as hard as you think it is,'* he says. *'You just need to have the belief, or,*

I don't know what it is, whether it's God or whether it's Buddha. I'm very simple. I just know, after I did these sort of things, life started to get a lot better.'

Brett had a Choice Point – a window of opportunity when he chose to do something different with his life. He chose to align with something much greater than himself.

Doing Whatever It Takes

Looking back on her life experiences, Barbara Marx Hubbard stresses that we have to make real changes to *ourselves,* to our lives, if we want to be the change. As we learned earlier, Barbara's purpose when she was younger had been to discover the meaning of new technology that was good. Later in her life, she raised five children, placing all thoughts of a career and a purpose behind her. But then, a new and renewed sense of purpose, an expansion of her earlier purpose, began to build in her, one that she knew she had to fully commit to.

'Very gradually, through a set of wonderful experiences, I realized my life purpose is to communicate humanity's potential to evolve; to communicate our potential to connect, and to be born as a more creative species,' she says. *'And once I got that, I crossed the Choice Point from making the choice, to actually doing something about it.'*

She knew she had to become the change; that she had to act on it. *'I had to move to Washington, D.C. and take my children with me. I had to get a divorce. And I had to say:*

"How can you start communicating positive options for the future?"' she explains. *'I couldn't do it where I was, or by doing what I did every day. I had to change what I did. I had to change where I lived, and then I had to gain new resources, find new friends. In order to be the change, you often have to change your life.'*

Barbara knew she had to become a complete match for what she wanted. But in doing so, she had to get into the flow of the current, and then she felt that the world worked with her, in support of her. *'If you do change your life along the direction of your deeper life purpose, you'll start to be rewarded, with your own expression, with your creativity, with feeling of service, of connecting with your colleagues and friends, and suddenly your life will take on so much more meaning, purpose and pleasure.'*

Making such life changes isn't always easy, of course. Often, it pushes us right out of our comfort zones. But the consequences of *not* living our purpose can be even more difficult, because we feel dissatisfied. *'What's really hard is not being the change,'* Barbara says. *'Not having a purpose. Because then all the modern symptoms of disease come up: depression, addiction, illnesses of all kinds, violence. If one is expressing one's creativity in alignment with others, there is much less tendency to be violent. So really, the solution is everybody finding that deeper life purpose and going for it.'*

Barbara recognizes that we don't all have the luxury or the opportunity to be the change, to commit to a sense of purpose. Often, we have financial or family obligations that need our attention. *'But hundreds of millions of us do,'* she points out. *'And if the ones that do have enough freedom and enough health to take a step to being the change, they start changing the whole world even for those who at this moment don't have that opportunity. The ones that can do it first have to move because that's the way the wave of evolution works. And those of us in the wave of change, have to be the change.'*

Birke Baehr also had to commit to being the change. He had to become a match for the change he wanted to see in the world. He tells us how, in the supermarket with his mum, he would question the food she was buying because through his research he had discovered that some products have traces of potentially harmful ingredients in them, or aren't sustainable for the planet. *'She'd put something in the cart and I'd pick it up and read the ingredients and I'd put it back,'* he says. *'When she asked me what I was doing, I'd say: "You can't buy that, it has high fructose corn syrup in it, or it has this in it, and that's bad for you." And I'd give her ten different reasons and all the side effects that have been proven by different labs and other things.'*

Using Your Skills for Good

'Success unshared is failure.' **John Paul DeJoria**

We all have skills, and there will always be ways in which we can apply them to making a positive difference. And when we do that, we make our own unique contribution to the world.

Richard Branson has turned his entrepreneurial skills toward making positive changes in the world. *'I spent the first half of my life building organizations for profit and now I suppose I am spending most of my time building organizations on a not-for-profit basis,'* he says. *'So I'm using my entrepreneurial skills to look at some of the intractable problems in the world and asking: "Can those problems be addressed in a better way?"'*

Richard was aware that Idi Amin had been persuaded by some tribal elders to step down as president of Uganda and go live out his life in Saudi Arabia, so he asked Nelson Mandela if he could speak with Saddam Hussein about doing something similar. He tells us the background: *'In the build-up to the Iraq War, I was feeling that the war would be an unjust one. All of us wanted to see Saddam Hussein step down, but to kill and maim thousands of people in the process did not seem like a good idea. So I contacted Nelson Mandela and asked him if he would consider going to see Saddam Hussein and try to persuade him to go and live in Libya for the rest of his life. And Mandela agreed to do that. He wanted Kofi Annan to go with him, and when he talked to Kofi, he agreed. They got on a plane to Johannesburg, but then, on the day they were due to go to Iraq, the bombing started and they never went.'*

The plan had been thwarted, but it was one that could really have made a difference. Then another idea emerged, inspired by musician Peter Gabriel, to establish a permanent group of 'Elders' – respected people with high moral authority who were no longer involved in politics who would attempt to intervene to diffuse conflict situations. Nelson Mandela agreed to be the Founding Elder and Graca Machel, his wife, agreed to work alongside him. Mandela then appointed 12 men and women from across the world – including Archbishop Desmond Tutu, Kofi Annan, former US president Jimmy Carter, Mary Robinson, and Ela Bhatt.

The Elders have worked behind the scenes to bring peace on a number of occasions. Richard describes some of their successes: *'Kofi Annan headed up a mission to Kenya with Archbishop Tutu and Graca Machel, trying to bring about an end to a very bloody civil war that erupted just after the elections there. They managed to get a coalition government formed in Kenya; and the country has been pretty peaceful since.*

'Behind the scenes they worked on trying to get the coalition government formed in Zimbabwe. It is not guaranteed that it will be as successful as Kenya's, but it has helped people in Zimbabwe quite considerably. The Elders have been working on the unification of Cyprus, too, and have made quite a few trips to Palestine and Israel, as one of their principal focuses is to try to get a Palestinian state formed and try and bring peace to the region.'

The True Purpose of Business

Richard has also been involved in setting up other inspiring change projects. *'We have done the same thing with the Carbon War Room,'* he says. *'We found an entrepreneurial person to run it. We set them up with the remit to try to get as much carbon out of the atmosphere as possible – to work with industry to try to get a gigatonne of carbon out of the shipping industry, a gigatonne of carbon out of the airline industry, and so on. And then we just gave them the independence to get on and do it.*

'We are setting up a centre for disease control in Africa, too. Of all the places in the world that need a centre for disease control, the only place that doesn't have one is Africa. We will set it up just like we would set up a business, except it could be set out to try to resolve a problem in an entrepreneurial way, rather than to make money.'

Richard offers some wisdom on the true purpose of business. *'As I have got older I have realized that governments come and governments go,'* he says. *'And the people who work in government come and go quite quickly. And therefore the responsibility, I think, comes onto the shoulders of business people, who may be there for 30, 40, 50, 60, 70 years, to play a major part. We set up Virgin Unite so we could unite all the people who work for Virgin in trying to make a real difference in the world. And I think that if every business took that approach, we could get on top of most of the major problems in the world.'*

Of course, businesses need to survive but they can still work toward making a positive difference, as Richard points out: *'I think that if somebody has just started building a business, the word 'survival' is critical, and therefore they can't spend too much time worrying about giving their money away. But what they can do is make sure they are running their business ethically and that, ideally, just through their business they are making a positive difference. That they are caring about the environment. That they can sleep well at night, because they know they are doing the right thing.*

'If they are doing the right thing, then all the people who work for them are going to be proud of the company and they are likely to work that little bit harder and so the company will do that little bit better. There will come a time when they start making money, and then they can perhaps turn their entrepreneurial skills into helping people less fortunate than themselves in the local community around their businesses. And if they become that much more successful, they can start turning to trying to help people in the wider world.'

And in this way, businesses definitely would be a force for good.

'Grow Appalachia'

John Paul DeJoria has turned his entrepreneurial skills toward helping some of his fellow Americans. Recognizing that there are hunger and food-security issues in some US states, he decided to help families in Appalachia, a region in the east of the country, to feed themselves. *'We started out at Grow Appalachia empowering families and individuals to take care of themselves, and then we empowered them to take care of their neighbors – to have the ability to do that,'* John Paul explains.

John Paul approached Berea College for help and paid for equipment, seeds, irrigation systems, fertilizer, and everything else the families needed in order to create their own vegetable gardens. *'We planted our first 100 gardens two years ago,'* he says. *'Some gardens were for one person, or one family, and were in the middle of nowhere. Others were for 50 families in one location: those were pretty big gardens. The end result was that, with the first 100 gardens, 2,700 people ate that year.'*

Then, as John Paul says, the families were *'smart enough to not only grow enough food for themselves, but enough to give some to their neighbors, who were good people, but destitute. They fed themselves and their neighbors, and then they canned the rest for the winter, when you can't grow anything. So now they can eat year round.'*

The project is on its way to meeting its target of feeding half of Appalachia within the next 5–7 years. On a recent visit, John Paul learned how the families are making a real success of their endeavors. He says: *'They were already growing extra vegetables and selling them to grocery stores locally, having little farmers' markets, and canning produce to start selling it so they can become an agricultural community. We treat them, give them all the equipment, give them all the seeds they want, and in return they can help some of their neighbors along the way.'* He adds, *'We're not giving away charity; we're helping people to help themselves.'*

The Social Entrepreneurs

We can think of Richard Branson and John Paul DeJoria as 'social entrepreneurs' – people who use their entrepreneurial skills to create and manage positive social changes. Bill Drayton, a social entrepreneur himself, founded an organization called Ashoka with the aim of finding such people all over the world and helping them to further their aims. It has been hugely successful, as Bill says: *'Over half the Ashoka fellows have changed national policy within 5 years of the organization's launch, and three-quarters have changed the pattern in their field at the national level within that time.'*

Bill shares with us a few examples of the work of Ashoka's social entrepreneurs. *'There is an African fellow who has discovered that the giant African rat has a really good sense of smell,'* he explains. *'It is better at detecting tuberculosis (TB) in spit samples than the labs are. The rats identify 40% more cases of TB than the lab technicians do, and they are much faster and much less expensive. Also, they are right there in the villages, where there are no labs.'*

Then there is the Bangladeshi man whose efforts became a national policy in his native country. *'He's a brilliant entrepreneur,'* says Bill. *'According to the UN evaluations, he has increased enrolment at school by 44%, cut the drop-out rate by half. His ideas have gone to India and Brazil, and officially become policy in Bangladesh. The students organize the extra sciences, grade them, help one another. The teacher goes from one small group of students to the next small group, as a resource. There's no homework, so the poor kids don't fall behind.'*

Through social entrepreneurship, thousands of lives around the world are being positively impacted. This is because, as Bill points out, social entrepreneurs are *'committed to the good of all.'*

A Foundation for Change

Like Richard Branson, John Paul DeJoria, and Bill Drayton, James Caan has also turned his skills toward making a positive difference in the world. He describes some of the work that his charitable foundation has been involved in. *'We set up the foundation and the first thing we did was build a school,'* he says. *'Then recently, there was a flood in Pakistan which affected 20 million people. I was watching the news and I just couldn't believe how so many people could be affected so quickly.*

'For some crazy reason, I felt that I wanted to go and see what had happened, so I did. When I arrived in Pakistan, I saw village after village where thousands of people had nothing. They'd lost their homes, they'd lost their livelihoods, they'd lost their cattle, they'd lost their farms. What had taken lifetimes and generations to accumulate had been lost in the space of seconds.'

When he returned, James set his foundation the task of reconstructing one of the villages that he had visited. The goal was immense, he says, and involved *'rebuilding something like 185 homes, the school, the hospital, the church, the mosque, the roads, the power, the drainage. I've never done anything like that in my life. Usually, calling out a plumber is a big challenge for me!'*

He reflects on the current state of the project, saying: *'We are almost 70% through the construction phase of the village and I am incredibly excited and very passionate that we will achieve what we set out to do, which is to give these people their lives back and put them back on the map as they were, before the floods happened.'*

James demonstrates what is possible when you align yourself completely with an idea and be the change. But you might be wondering what *you* can do to make a positive difference. Richard, James, John Paul, and Bill had resources and connections that enabled them to make great impressions, but they built those up from being a match for making a positive difference. And you can make a start down that road if you choose to.

Fairness: Best for Everyone Involved

'The problem with winning is somebody has to lose, which means it becomes a transaction and not a relationship, and therefore it is not sustainable.' JAMES CAAN

Speaking with James Caan, it became clear that he has built his career around some core principles that he absorbed from watching his father. These principles were based on fairness and honesty, and by running his own businesses in this kind of way, James has made a difference.

'I learned very early on that business is very much about relationships, and not about transactions, and in order to build relationships you have to be conscious of the fact that in a business deal you have to find what is right for you, but also what is right for the other side,' says James.

'I discovered that if you could create a business transaction where both parties felt they had won from the deal, then you would have the foundations of building a much longer term relationship than doing a transaction that is all about winning.'

James tells us about an occasion when his father had negotiated a price with a supplier, but then stopped to consider whether the price was fair: *'The price that the supplier quoted my father was too little, and I was sitting there with a bit of a smile on my face thinking he had got a really good deal. Go, Dad! Then, to my shock and horror, my father stopped and asked the supplier: "Are you happy with that?" And the man smiled and said, "Actually, no, because there is no margin in it for me."*

'My father wanted to build a relationship with that supplier because he felt he had the right products of the right quality so he asked him: "What would be a fair price that would give you a reasonable margin, but also allows me to come back and justify that price?" And the supplier increased the price by 10–15%, which, in my father's eyes, didn't really make a lot of difference. Yet it did make a difference to the supplier, who was now able to charge a margin that made him a profit from the deal.'

James's father explained to him that building positive relationships meant long-term sustainability and success – all his father's customers and suppliers stayed with him throughout his entire career. James notes that this kind of moral principle has been rather forgotten these days. *'Business today is so transaction focused,'* he says. *'It is all about the deal now. Everything around me is very much driven by short-term thinking, whereas when I was growing up, it wasn't like that. It felt like businesses were built on serving a community, or serving a market, or serving a sector and building a reputation.'*

This principle, and the overall importance of being good and fair, is what James has *become* in his life. Living these principles – aligning with harmonious patterns and thus exchanging information with them – has led him to be presented with even bigger and more harmonious opportunities, which have culminated in his entry into the world of philanthropy, an area that he now devotes much of his time to.

THINGS TO REMEMBER

---

1. We sometimes have to make significant personal changes in order to change our lives, or the world.

2. We can turn our own skills toward making a positive difference.

3. Everyone can make a positive difference.

4. Transactions and deals are examples of short-term thinking. Fairness produces stronger relationships and long-term results.

CHAPTER 9

TOWARD A BETTER WORLD

'I truly believe that changing the life of one person is like changing the life of a nation. Everything has to have a beginning, and I think if we don't start the process, if people don't embark on the journey, then where is the destination? Where are we going?'

JAMES CAAN

Based on what we have learned so far, it makes sense that a solution to many of the world's problems would be to share more, both in our lives and in the world. That means more generosity in the sharing of our resources, of ourselves, of our time and effort. And we need to believe that our efforts will be fruitful, that they are not small and insignificant, and that we can all make a difference. As Alison Pothier says: *'In order for the world to become the generosity that it wants to receive, the world inside has to shift to trust and believe that that is possible in order to make that change.'*

This is why we have explored some scientific principles in this book – to help you to understand that everything is connected, and that every act has consequences. So where do we start?

James Caan believes that if we all do a little, it can go a long way: *'I don't think the issues of the world are really down to a handful of people,'* he says. *'It is about society recognizing and accepting that we all have our own little responsibilities, whether we give £5 a month or £10 a month. I think the gesture is a place to start because it gets you on the journey. It is having the inclination, the want, and the determination to do something for somebody else, whether that's a gesture, helping out an old person, doing shopping for somebody who can't do it for themselves, or looking after somebody's child. It is the beginning of a journey. Once you start and you realize the difference you can make, it goes a long way.'*

It Doesn't Take Much to Change Someone's Life

'If everybody in the world tried to make a difference, then the world could be a much happier place than it has been in the past.' **RICHARD BRANSON**

Richard Branson encourages us to realize that gestures that might seem small to us can have a transformational effect on those who most need that help. *'I think everybody can make a difference in the world, some obviously only in quite a small way, others in a bigger way,'* he says.

Richard gives an example of how we could make such a difference. In the developing world, mainly in Africa, many pregnant women, especially young girls, suffer prolonged or complicated labor and childbirth and this can lead to obstetric fistulas – a hole between the vagina and the bladder that causes leakage and infections. Fistulas carry great social stigma and the women are often ostracized by their families and communities. Yet fistulas can be repaired in a simple operation that costs just $150.

Let's put this into perspective. Many people in the world can't afford to donate $150, but many can. Consider what it would mean if you forwent new clothes or music for a few months, and instead used the money to change someone's life. Your own life might never be the same again as you come to that recognition. *'Pretty much everyone in the world is in a position where they are capable of radically changing somebody else's life,'* says Richard.

We think that happiness comes from possessions or achievements, but deep happiness can be a product of what we do for others. Richard believes that *'people get the greatest satisfaction in life from making a difference to other people's lives. And it's not until you actually start trying to do this that you realize the enormous satisfaction it will give you.'* It doesn't have to be $150. All it takes to start is a gesture, something that is possible for you.

Learning It at School

'It's like being a brilliant cello player – you have to practice it. You can't have a concept of being a brilliant cello player. Same thing with being a good person. You have to have the skill – you have to practice it.' **BILL DRAYTON**

Empathy is where the willingness to help others begins. Bill Drayton gives us an inspiring example of the teaching of empathy in schools. He describes an innovative program developed by one of his Ashoka fellows, Marianne Gordon, who spent some time teaching in a school in Toronto, Canada. Marianne observed that some of the children didn't know how to respond to classmates who made them uncomfortable, other than through aggression. Which, as Bill says, *'invites aggression back, and every time you go through that cycle it gets deeper, and the likelihood of those children being able to contribute to society is proportionately going down.'*

Marianne found a solution to this problem – by starting a program to teach empathy. Bill explains what she did: *'She brought a baby to the class once a month. The baby was under the age of one and he wore a T-shirt with the words "The Professor" on it. He came in with mum, occasionally dad. The kids surrounded "The Professor" and they were asked to find out what "The Professor" was saying and what "The Professor" was feeling. These were exercises and reflections. Within 25–30 hours, the children grasped this fundamental skill.'*

Marianne's program has been so successful that, as Bill proudly points out, *'she has gone from 2 to 14,000 schools in seven countries, and it's growing fast.'* One of the measurable benefits of it is that *'bullying rates have come down and stayed down.'*

Learning the skill of empathy is vital for children, and it

gives them an invaluable tool for their future – one that will benefit all of us as they learn to function more effectively in a changing world. If we develop empathy and learn to help others when we are children, then it becomes a natural thing for us as we get older.

That's a belief that John Paul DeJoria shares. At the Paul Mitchell schools he established, helping others is part of the training. *'We have about 15,000 students in the US, in 110 schools,'* he says. *'Part of their culture, their curriculum, is to raise money to help their own community, their own state, our country, and the world. Part of their curriculum is giving back and how good it makes them feel, and that's why they do it. And they go forth and tell others, and in this way we spread this good energy.'*

Little Things Count

'I think small gestures are critical.' **PETER BUFFETT**

We can start to look at how we lead our lives right now and make some small, but practical, changes. Peter Buffett suggests that these can just be in how we recognize others, or recognize their roles: *'Philanthropy means the love of people,'* he reminds us. *'It doesn't mean you have a big foundation and are giving a bunch of money. So philanthropy can work every single day. When I go to my local coffee store and I acknowledge the person behind the counter, ask them how their day is going, or if I just recognize them as a human being. It is sad, actually, when they come back* and say: "Wow, nobody has even seen me today." Every little gesture can mean so much.'

John Paul DeJoria says: 'You don't have to be a politician, you don't have to be a wealthy person, you don't have to be in power. You can be any living thing in this world and if you just walk down the street and smile at someone coming your way, you're already exchanging happiness and giving out the love. If you see someone who needs a helping hand, you don't need money to do it – just put yourself there and give them a helping hand.'

Bill Drayton encourages all of us to become change-makers – people who make positive changes around them that benefit others. He says, 'All of us can make a difference. Once we define ourselves as a change-maker, we become like smart white blood cells as we live our lives. Wherever we go, we see something that is stuck, that's a mess, and say, "Ah, that's an opportunity for me to express love and respect in action. I can solve this problem."'

Bill encourages parents to help their children to think like this, too. Not only will it make a positive difference, but the kids can develop empathy and other skills that will help them throughout their lives. He offers the following example of how to do this: 'If you have a 15 year old and he says that the poor kids in the neighborhood can't play sports because they don't have equipment, you have a God-given opportunity to say to him: "Why don't you get your friends together and find a solution?"

He might say, "What?!" But you can say, "Yes, you can do this and by the way, this is the most important thing you can do. Forget piano lessons. This is really important because this is what is going to give you critical skills, and you are going to be helping all your friends get these skills. This is what the world really requires."'

Peter Buffet suggests that we look at making positive changes even in the smaller things in our own lives, in our daily behaviors, and that we address any misalignment that we find. 'I talk about self-reflection,' he says. 'It is like looking at yourself and saying: "OK, am I aligned with what I am saying I am, or what I want to be or do in the world?" I don't know if you can be 100% aligned – in fact I am pretty sure you can't, because when I go to the store, I buy things and they stick them in plastic bags and I am out in the world singing about how terrible plastic is. I'm being a hypocrite!

'So the next time I go to the store I buy a reusable bag and I start to change my behavior. And that happens every day in so many ways. You can't beat yourself up about it, but you do have to examine it and ask, "Where can I shift my behavior so I am aligned with what I say, am, or want to be – or want others to be?" And that is a constant work in progress.'

What Each of Us Can Do

Jack Canfield makes a similar point about environmental sustainability and how the change has to start with each of us, in our own small ways: 'Recently, a Choice Point for me was about ecological sustainability – examining my *own lifestyle and looking at how much consumption was involved in that, and how there was an underlying belief that "more is better," whether it was more purchasing, creating a better economy, owning more stuff.*

'Looking at the consumption of oil and energy and all that was a very confrontational moment in time for me: to really look at myself and say: "OK, if I'm going be part of a solution and not part of the problem, I've got to change my behavior. I need to have a zero carbon footprint on the planet, and things like that."' He points out that it's *'not cheap to do that, either. I had to make some choices that have actually cost me more money. So that was an important Choice Point for me.'*

Small behavioral changes like the ones Jack describes can mark the start of *being* the change that will enable us to create a more environmentally sustainable world. There are many, many things we can do. Here, Jack shares some examples from his own life with us: *'I plan my trips in the car; I walk more; I turn the water off in the middle of my shower, soap up and then turn it back on again when I'm done so I use less hot water. And I don't let the water run in the sink when we are doing the dishes. We use canvas bags when we go shopping. We're recycling pretty much everything we can, and reusing what we can. I still drink water out of bottles occasionally, plastic bottles, but very rarely. I have several stainless steel bottles that I carry water around in.*

'We're looking at solar panels for the property. And we're doing carbon offsets, so when I travel by air, we buy credits

for the places where they're creating buildings for cows, to capture the gas so it doesn't go up and affect the biosphere. These are little things but they all add up.' He places great importance on this maxim. 'I don't want to sit here and know that my grandchildren won't have a planet because I'm being over-consumptive,' he says.

And Birke Baehr, one of the younger generation of people committed to a sustainable future, also encourages us to take the necessary action. 'The answer to all this pollution and everything that's wrong is to start taking the steps,' he says. 'We need to start doing more research, like back when I was eight and I started doing the research, learning more about it, then finally I took the steps and started eating organic. And now when I open up the fridge, everything I see in there is 100% organic, because that's how I know you can have real, clean, healthy, sustainable food.'

And leaders of businesses can work to make their businesses sustainable, too. John Paul DeJoria explains how he runs his businesses. 'We're 100% carbon neutral,' he says. 'Sustainability is taking nature and all living forms and maintaining the healthy balance between them. You pollute too much water, you're gonna really hurt all living forms. You pollute the air, you're hurting all living forms. How to balance it? We plant more trees than all the carbon we use. If we do a big seminar, whatever it took to put on that big seminar, we plant more trees than all the carbon we use. We're making sure our planet is here for us and many future generations.'

John Paul gives us a simple metaphor for how we can live with nature and without exploiting it: *'As the river flows, it goes around rocks, it goes around mountains, but it continues, it doesn't stop. You may see the river go all over the place, but eventually it goes in harmony and it maintains itself. If, through life, you go along with the harmony of life and let it be itself, you are going through it like the river. You're flowing along, not hurting anything at all, going around it, helping it out, and still reaching your destination and maintaining the flow to that destination.'*

All Together Now

"Children learn that being part of a family means working together as a team. And I do believe that that's probably one of the most important life lessons that we can teach, that they aren't alone, that it's not about them, that it's about all of us."
JODI ORTON

We are in this world together and the greatest changes will occur when we *all* get behind them. If we want to see more compassion in the world then we need to show greater compassion toward each other. If we want to see more forgiveness, then that also starts with each of us.

Richard Branson believes that success is actually reliant on how well you deal with people. *'I think the most successful people are those who are good at dealing properly with people, dealing well with people; people who genuinely* care about others, people who are good at bringing out *the best in others. And I think those are the people who, generally speaking, end up being successful in life,'* he says, before adding: *'So I think you might get lucky if you are an unpleasant bastard, but I don't think that is the way to become successful in life.'*

In other words, being an 'unpleasant bastard' might get you results in the short term, but it is definitely not the way to get them in the long term. Being unpleasant doesn't help us to align with harmonious patterns, either, so most of what we attempt to accomplish will either fail over time, or will take a lot more effort than it needs to.

We all share this world. Life needn't be about personal or corporate gain. For when we view it that way, if somebody wins, somebody else has to lose. That might be OK in sport, but in life, cooperation is key. We need to work together. What would it be like if nobody had to lose, if instead we helped each other to win? Our relationships with each other are our keys to the future. In scientific terms, life relies on information exchange and thus on relationships between things. In personal terms, everything relies on our relationships and the exchanges between us.

Building Positive Relationships

To get to this place, we need to challenge some of our core assumptions. One of these is the idea that humans are inherently selfish, that self-interest is our nature. This assumption lies at the heart of economics and business and because of it, many corporations seek to gain at the expense of the world. But we need to rise above self-interest. We need to seek out the common good and work toward building a future for all of us.

That is the challenge, and the answer lies in reminding ourselves that we are actually not self-interested. In fact, we are wired for cooperation, compassion, and kindness, and when we act on these attributes, we *all* gain. So we should seek to create positive relationships because they are the basis for cooperation. This means strengthening those that we already have, and even mending fences where relationships have broken down.

Richard Branson recognized that it was very important to repair his relationship with British Airways after he had a dispute with them. *'One thing I have learned is life is too short to fall out with anybody,'* he says. *'And if you do have a relationship clash, or a divorce, or something serious in your life, the most important thing is to befriend your enemy, however difficult that may be. Befriend the people you have fallen out with.'* We should aim to mend fences, then, instead of seeking some form of payback. *'I am absolutely certain the world would be a far better place if it was run based more on forgiveness,'* Richard adds.

Richard nominates Nelson Mandela as a model for this, because, after spending nearly three decades in prison, he forgave his captors, brought them into his fold, and worked with them. He had a greater vision of a united South Africa and a deep understanding that in order to make such a thing happen, forgiveness and reconciliation had to be a fundamental part of who he was. *'I had the privilege of getting to know Nelson Mandela. And he and the people around him, I suspect, are the greatest examples of people who've learned the art of forgiveness. And that forgiveness sent out a tremendous example to the rest of the world,'* says Richard.

Forgiving and Moving On

Richard also describes how Mandela's countryman Archbishop Desmond Tutu presided over a court-like restorative justice body in South Africa after the end of apartheid: *'Instead of presiding over a court to hang or execute people, as would happen, I am afraid, in some Western countries, he presided over the Court of Truth and Reconciliation, where those people who had sinned against the black person came to the court and had to confront the relatives of the people they had sinned against, and ask for forgiveness. And on that basis Archbishop Tutu forgave them, and the relatives forgave them, and the country was able to move on.'*

You might argue that we need to have punishment and, of course, there are a great many crimes where that is the most appropriate course of action. But there are also a great many others where a better way would be the encouragement of forgiveness, with some act of atonement – perhaps involving an act of visible social payback. When we forgive, we set ourselves free. Then we can all move forward. In the end, we are all in this together, and it is vital to remember that we are all connected. As Archbishop Desmond Tutu says: *'We look for a glorious dénouement, when we will discover that we are actually members of one family.'*

Tony Benn shares a revealing example of this inter-connectedness: *'I once worked out a very simple calculation,'* he says. *'We have two parents, four grandparents, eight great grandparents, 16 great, great grandparents and 32 great, great, great grandparents. So every generation, which lasts for about 25 years, you double the number of ancestors we have.*

'I worked out very carefully how many ancestors I had. I can't remember the outcome, but I think if I go back 2,000 years, I have 9,000 billion ancestors or something unbelievable. You can work it out for yourself! And since there weren't that number of people in the world at the time, it must mean we are all interconnected. And therefore everyone is a cousin. I could say to you, "Dear cousin." And if we went back, we could find the moment when our families interconnected. And that, I think, is a statistical way of confirming the idea that the human family is a family that has a common interest in survival.'

In an echo of Archbishop Tutu's sentiment, Tony adds: *'Nationality, which has been the source of a lot of conflict in the past, is being replaced by an awareness that we are all members of the human race.'* The younger generation, he says, doesn't have the same sense of national divisions that we have, and therefore there is hope for us all. *'If I talk to my granddaughters, who are 15 and 13, about multiculturalism they don't understand what I'm talking about because they are at a school with 76 different nationalities.*

'When I used to go to the school to speak, it was like addressing a General Assembly of the UN. They have Muslim, French, and Jewish friends; American friends, Jamaican friends. And for them, they are members of the human race. 'So I think the younger generation, because of technology, have come to appreciate very important lessons about the world in which they live.'

From Crisis to Transformation

'My metaphor is this: our crisis is a birth.'
BARBARA MARX HUBBARD

It's easy to be pessimistic about some of the world's problems, and feel that everything is going to fall apart. But Jack Canfield says that we should see this as the beginning of something new – as a natural process of chaos that precedes something better: *'Some of us have had the experience of remodeling a home, and before it gets better, it gets worse. They come in, they tear out the bathroom or the kitchen. There is dust everywhere, plastic sheets hanging down, and you are cooking outside on a butane stove. You wonder if it's ever going to end. But when it's all finished you have a much more harmonious home: updated, functional, and effective.'*

He likens the process to childbirth. *'Change is messy. Birth is messy,'* he says. *'I actually delivered two of my own children. I'm not a doctor, but I studied the subject and I wanted to be there; I didn't want it to be in a hospital, I wanted it to be more organic. And you know, blood happens and everything is sticky and people scream, and so on. But once it's over, you get this beautiful baby and after a while, the pain of the birth is over and life goes on.'*

Jack encourages us not to shy away from change, and to realize that chaos before a change is the natural course of things. *'So you have to be willing to go through the chaos in order for it to reorganize at a higher level. Now that's the thing to remember. That it goes: here is a structure, it gets dissolved and then it reformulates at a higher level of integration. And that's really what we're always after. We want to take it to a new level, but we sometimes have to destroy what is in order to take it to the higher level.'*

There's a nice example of this in the process used to purify chemical compounds, some of which are medicines. An impure material is dissolved in a solvent, like alcohol, and then the solvent is slowly evaporated. During the evaporation, the compound reorganizes itself into a highly pure, crystalline material. And the crystals are in a much more organized state than the initial material.

If we can get comfortable with the idea that change is inevitable, that it can be messy, that we sometimes have to dissolve the old ways to create better ways, we can make some peace with it and the change process becomes easier for us. Jack talks about the changes that are taking place in the world's systems: *'I believe that where we are in history right now, there is a lot of conflict, a lot of breaking down of systems,'* he says. *'We see it in economic systems. We see possible meltdown in places like Greece, and Portugal, and Ireland; perhaps the whole of Europe is going to be restructured. I think the American system is deadlocked right now, nothing much is happening. We saw the breakdown of the financial system and all those sorts of things just fell apart. It didn't work.'*

He believes that we are going to see a lot more breakdown in the systems we've come to rely on – from financial systems and currency to forms of government. *'And I think that's OK,'* he insists, *'because something higher is going to come out of that. It is going to be painful for a while. There are going to be some austerity measures and it is nothing that anybody wants but the fact is, humanity as a whole is going to come to a much higher place.'*

A Social Butterfly

When we understand that this process is natural, we can feel more confident that despite the difficulties, we will emerge from the chaos to a much better place. We need to be optimistic, though, Barbara Marx Hubbard says, so we can make the best possible choices: *'A lot of people I know are pessimistic. They are saying, "I don't think the human species is going to make it; I don't think we are smart enough; I think we are too selfish." And there is a lot of it that's true. But unless you see that crises precede transformation, you won't be able to look for what's innovative and creative. And then your own Choice Point is affected by the fact that you feel you're part of a positive potential.'*

Barbara builds upon this sense of optimism by drawing a parallel between our current situation and the metamorphosis of a caterpillar into a butterfly: *'The body of the caterpillar, at a certain point, gets bloated; it overeats and can't continue to grow. Meanwhile, inside the caterpillar are "imaginal" cells. They have an image, an image of what's coming, you could say. And they start to proliferate and they find each other.*

'The imaginal cells look foreign, though, so the body of the caterpillar tries to destroy them. But they keep on growing, because it's part of the pattern. And at some point, the caterpillar literally disappears and those cells find themselves in a chrysalis, building a new body. So these little cells that looked like they were going to be destroyed, and many of them were, hold within them their part in building something new. So if you could look inside a chrysalis, you'd see: there is the antenna, there somebody is building the wings, there is the whole body.'

Nature has a goal, she says, and that *'at some point, the whole body is ready and it's a new butterfly. It pops out of the chrysalis and there it is: a wet-winged butterfly that can't quite fly yet. So nature has a pattern there. It's a metamorphosis – the change in form from the caterpillar to the butterfly.'*

Barbara likens the caterpillar's metamorphosis to societal change. *'Now the analogy here,'* she says, *'is we're going to have a change in the form of our societies: from competitive, top-down structures with all the separate disciplines, to the one that we are building right now for all these Choice Points. That society would be more creative, more just, more peaceful. Not a utopia, not perfect, but we'd be over the problems of separation and deficiency, and into the possibilities of creativity and potential. And we'd have a whole new set of crises and problems, because it's ever evolving.*

'So I'm not speaking here of creating some perfect society, but shifting from this set of problems to a far higher order. And so the butterfly is out and I think, within our lifetimes, there's going to be a visible social butterfly, made up of all the Choice Points of all the imaginal cells in the social body that are choosing to be something more positive.'

Leading the Change

Robert E. Quinn also says that a hierarchical, top-down structure in society won't work if we want real change. He favors the idea of 'transformational leadership' – where we lead by example, and those who are inspired by our example become leaders themselves and help further the cause, leading to a transformation in society. In this way, as we lead by being the change, the systems in the world begin to change around us.

And the call for this doesn't come from the top. It starts with anyone who decides to change him- or herself. When we lead by example because we have a vision for a better way, we embrace an authentic power inside us because we are aligned with something greater than ourselves. In this way, how our lives run is no longer determined by those at the top – those who have historically created the systems – with rules and instructions filtering down to us. As *we* change, the systems change.

Robert says that *'The fundamental assumption we find everywhere is that macro determines micro – the big systems turn the little ones.'* But with transformational leadership, there is *'an exceptional moment where one person changes the whole system. It's micro determining macro. When we are in a fundamental state of leadership, when we claim who we really are, we turn the world upside down. We gain the power, we gain the freedom, we gain the strength to make the world change according to where it actually needs to go because we can see where it needs to go.'*

Robert helps us realize that the world can change when we change. That's the way it's always been and always will be. And how better to change than to embrace the power of love.

THINGS TO REMEMBER

1. Every one of us matters.

2. Small gestures can go a long way.

3. It doesn't take much to change someone's life.

4. There are many things we can do in our own lives to help create a more sustainable future.

5. We're all in this together.

6. Good relationships are important.

7. Crises precede transformation.

8. When we change ourselves and embrace our inner power, we can change the world.

CHAPTER 10

THE POWER OF LOVE

'The secret is not what you want to get,
but what you want to give.'

BARBARA MARX HUBBARD

Will we choose the power of love or the love of power? John Paul DeJoria offers us some simple advice on how we choose the power of love: *'The way you do that is you start doing something that benefits others, without wanting anything in return.'*

We believe that many of the problems in today's world are a result of our love of power. But if we want to change our world, we need to flip this over and cultivate the power of love instead. Scilla Elworthy says: *'Power from within is infinite. There is no end to it. Whereas power in the world is limited.'* There will always be a limit to external power – whether it is financially, in property, in possessions, in control over others – but inner power, the power of love, is endless.

'There is a limit to the amount of money anyone can accumulate,' Scilla says. And expanding on this idea, *'There*

is a limit to the number of troops, or votes, or weapons you can have, whereas the power that is available from within is literally infinite. You see it in somebody like Nelson Mandela or Desmond Tutu or Aung San Suu Kyi: that incredible power of inspiration in one human being that enables other human beings to be the best they can be.

'That is the genius of the great peace-builders and the great mediators: that whoever they are talking to, even if it is a serial killer or somebody who has tortured people, they still seek the goodness within that person, and find it. It requires patience and tolerance and compassion to do that, but they find what they are looking for in that person.'

Love Is Natural to Us

'They say angels fly because they take themselves lightly.'
SCILLA ELWORTHY

Love is innate in all of us. It is our strongest legacy, our deepest yearning, and it is our greatest power. It is priceless. Jodi Orton says, *'The awards, the accolades, they don't mean a thing when my son or my daughter comes home at the end of the day and still gives me a kiss on the cheek. You just can't put a price on that.'*

The magic of love is that it's already inside us. We needn't ever have to wait for something to happen for us to express it. It's ours to share at any time. It can just be in a warm, heartfelt smile. It can be a gentle hand on the shoulder or

192

a compassionate squeeze of the arm. We can find it in the eyes of a loved one. It can be in an affectionate kiss or a hug. Many would agree that the three most powerful words in the universe are: 'I love you.' James Caan says: *'To me, love is about swimming the second mile. It is always doing that one thing extra that kind of quantifies and illustrates and demonstrates the strength of that emotion.'*

Love can be in a thought that brings a smile to the face and a warm feeling in the heart. It can be breakfast in bed or a cup of tea at the end of a long day. It can be carried on a compliment or in a simple gesture of thanks. We can express it in gratitude. Love's power is inexhaustible.

It can be like turning on the light in a dark room. It illuminates everything. And it does so without preference. It does not choose sides. It does not recognize obstacles. It pays no attention to color, creed, nor religion. We are all equal in love's eyes.

The moment we choose love, we begin the process of moving toward a better world because we create the world from the inside out. Love reflects who we are. It frees us and so it frees the world. It elevates us and it gives others wings to rise up and be all they've ever dreamed they could be.

Scilla Elworthy reveals how simple it can be to show love. *'You might be on a train or a bus and there is a child crying,'* she says. *'And instead of getting irritated that the child is making such a noise, you actually just take the child into your heart – in a way, cuddle it. You will find the child will stop crying, even though you may be five seats away. But you kind of give him or her some warmth and you will notice it stops crying. The child will get it. Children do.'*

She then encourages us to be mindful of opportunities to love and give them precedence over some of the smaller things in our lives. *'Instead of being constantly obsessed with ourselves – have I got the right shoes and can I afford this or that,'* she says, *'we can broaden the picture to the other people on the bus, or people at work who are struggling, or the person who constantly doesn't feel she looks good enough. And a hand goes out, or a very positive comment, or something that makes life a bit nicer, more worth living.'*

Needing Nothing in Return

John Paul DeJoria tells us how, in 1982, he acted on an opportunity to help a woman with a group of children. His company had just paid their bills on time for the first time ever. They had $2,000 in the bank so John Paul decided to take a friend out to a Mexican restaurant to celebrate. He describes how he encountered the woman and the kids.

'There was a table 9 feet from me with a dozen inner-city children and a lady looking at the menu,' he recalls. *'I knew they were from the inner city because I'm from the inner city. The kids had ragged clothes on. You knew their shoes probably didn't fit that well. It was some special occasion. I don't know what made me do this, but I walked into the kitchen behind the waiter – we had the same waiter – and I*

counted, 12 kids, 2 adults, right, what's the worst they could do? It's a couple hundred dollars. I could afford that. I told the waiter: "Give them anything they want and I'll give you a 15% tip." And that was big for me in those days because I wasn't used to having money. Then I said: "But don't tell them who did it."

'I went back to my table and sat down,' John Paul continues. *'The waiter told the lady and she said, "You're kidding! Really?" The waiter said, "Yes, and he's gonna pay for the tip also, a person in here." This lady stands up turns around, looks at me – it can't be this guy, she thinks. She slowly goes around the room – it's a big restaurant – trying to find a person who is looking at her, or who this can be. So she's standing in front of me, now she's 3 feet from me, and with this big angelic voice, she says loudly: "Whoever you are, God bless you, you have no idea what you are doing for me and these children!"*

She never knew who did it. I walked on a cloud for a couple of days. Giving back, asking nothing in return, and seeing the reaction you get by that choice is priceless. And there's no question that somewhere along the way those kids and that lady will do something good for somebody else and they know that there's love, she was given love, and there's love out there.'

It's About the Heart, Not the Head

Every situation, despite its clothing, presents us with an opportunity to love. When life challenges us, it's not always about trying to create something else, trying to find a way out or creating something bigger and grander in our lives. It's about taking the situation facing us right now and asking: "How can I love more right now? How can I be more kind, gentle, or compassionate?"

If you can love, you have succeeded in life. A worthy pursuit in life would be to remove all of our inner obstacles to love, all of the reasons and excuses that we create for not showing love in every moment of every day in our lives. To love is the most important thing we can ever do.

Jodi Orton describes the feeling she gets when a child who has not known love before finally opens up: *'There is more power when a child reaches out to you and takes down a wall, and accepts that touch, and accepts it selflessly and unconditionally, than all the money in the world. There aren't enough dollars, pennies, pounds, lira, rubles – there's just not enough money in the world to re-create that moment. And if you're really lucky, you'll see that moment over and over and over again.'*

Robert E. Quinn remembers preparing a class for his students that was around understanding the importance of love, connection, and moving toward a higher good. He'd written a discussion question on the film *A Man for All Seasons*, which is about Sir Thomas More, the man who refused to endorse England's King Henry VIII's wish to divorce his wife. Robert explains the message behind the question: *'In the Tower of London, Sir Thomas More is about to die and they send his family in. His daughter Meg tries to pose some rational arguments about why he should give in. And he responds with some rational arguments. They reach an impasse and More says: "Meg, in the end it is not about reason, it is about love."*

'I believe we spend our whole lives in the world of rhetoric and argument and what Thomas More is saying is that in the end, it is about the connections and the harmony. It is about the heart, not the head. Because the consequence of just using our heads is that we use them to rationalize and to justify and to live in our negativity; we destroy the fabric of the harmony, the fabric of the connections. But it is in being connected and moving toward that higher good that the universe manifests itself, that the energy flows, that people flourish. And I think that is what it is all about.'

Scilla Elworthy shares a moving example of the power of love. *'I was in Israel with a group of German people,'* she recalls. *'They were second generation from Nazi forebears. The Israelis they met had grandparents who had been in the concentration camps. So here were the German descendants of the perpetrators, and the Israeli descendants of the victims.*

'And they met and talked together in one-on-one conversations and inevitably, they ended up in tears because the question they asked was: "What is left to be healed?" And they found it instantly because they approached it like that.'

She describes the transformation in the room as everyone began to share a powerful connection. *'After that, as a form of reflection or meditation if you like, the whole group started to hum. Just humming. And as they hummed together, a sort of swirling started to happen. Different notes introduced themselves – how, I don't know – so that the sound moved almost like the chorus in Handel's* Messiah. *It just sounded up. People started to open their mouths and sing. But they were singing together... and I was astonished at the beauty of what came out of their mouths together.'*

We're All the Same, Really

Love and connecting with each other is what we're all about. Robert E. Quinn believes that love helps us break down barriers and get through to everyone. Using an example of the training of teachers, he says: *'When you are in school, they teach you how to teach and that all students are the same. Then you start your job and you discover every student is different, and you have to figure out how to reach all these different kids. And that makes you a better teacher.*

'But then you discover that every kid is the same after all. What kind of paradox is this?! And when you discover that every kid wants to be loved, no matter what they say or how they behave, and every kid wants to succeed, no matter what they say, then you can go into the inner city and teach those kids and succeed. You can go to the suburban district and teach those kids and succeed. You can teach the adults, you can teach anybody.

'You discover that there is a common code and you teach to those needs and interests,' he continues. *'That's deep*

wisdom, and it's true all over the world. It's a universal theory. That's Advance Change Theory. That's the fundamental state of leadership.'

He explains that the essence of Advance Change Theory is that *'we change the world by changing ourselves.'* And in changing ourselves, we become those higher principles that have their basis in the power of love.

Inspiring Lessons from the Past

'We must be the change we want to see in the world.'
MOHANDAS GANDHI

Robert E. Quinn recalls a powerful scene in the 1982 film of the life of Gandhi that demonstrates the importance of the great man's core principles, which were based on the power of love. Gandhi is on a hunger strike, Robert says, when *'a man comes up, pulls a piece of bread out of his shirt, throws it on Gandhi's chest and says "Take it, eat it, I'm going to hell but not with your death on my conscience."*

'Gandhi looks at the man and says, "Only God decides who goes to hell."

'The man replies angrily: "I took a child and I bashed its brains against a wall. They, the Muslims, they killed my little boy."

'Gandhi thinks for a moment and then he says, "I know a way out of hell." The man looks shocked. And Gandhi

continues, "Find a little boy whose mother and father have been killed, and raise him as your own." The man has this look, and he's paying attention and you can see this little ray of hope.

'And then Gandhi says, "Only, be sure he is a Muslim boy and that you raise him as one." The man looks like he is on the verge of shattering, this image is so repulsive to him. And he turns and he walks away. 'He takes three steps and then he freezes and turns back. He looks at Gandhi and he falls on his knees and he begins to cry.'

The man is crying, Robert explains, *'because he just went through a little atonement, a little transformation. And he's found a way out of hell.'*

The power of love offered him a way out of hell.

'Where did Gandhi get that?' Robert marvels. *'Was that in the script he had prepared? It was because he internalized a set of principles that were so real to him, and they operated, and they were so powerful he could use them anywhere, and at any time.'* When you work from the power of love you don't need a script, and Gandhi's principles were based on the power of love.

Robert also offers a lesson from the life of Martin Luther King. On the night before a major march, he explains, King received a phone call – it was a death threat from a racist who said: *'You will be sorry you came to this town because you are never leaving it.'*

But, Robert says, King chose the power of love: *'King hangs up the phone, his knees turn to jelly, his stomach fills with panic. He is full of terror, but he gets down on his knees and he prays and he says: "Tomorrow there's a march, thousands of people have come. If I don't have courage, they will not have courage." And he asks for courage for them; that he'd have courage so they could have courage.'*

The power of love gave Martin Luther King the courage he needed that night. Robert also cites the example shown by other inspirational teachers, such as Nelson Mandela and Victor Frankl, a survivor of the concentration camp at Auschwitz. *'There's always someone on the edge,'* he says, *'choosing to live those higher principles no matter how hard the context.'*

We can be inspired by such figures, and we can learn from them. We can put their teachings into practice in our own lives. We all have the ability to love, to care, to show compassion. Scilla Elworthy asks us to consider this: *'The qualities we read about in the greats, can we have those same qualities? Can we teach ourselves? Of course we can.'*

Love Is the Way

Love is central to all the world's religions. James Caan says that, despite the differences between religions, love and peace are the main teachings of them all. He describes how he attended an event, where there was *'somebody representing Islam, somebody representing Christianity, and somebody representing Judaism.'*

He was expecting quite a bit of conflict and disagreement, he says, but *'to my absolute amazement, I got there and there was no drama because they all believed in exactly the same things. All the religions really believe in the same essence, which is about peace. It is about being good to your neighbor. It is about giving something back.'*

James believes that much of the religious conflict we see is caused by what we construct around the religious teachings. *'If you take the fundamental principles of most religions,'* he points out, *'the message is the same. They just communicate it in a different way. And I think what creates most conflict around the world isn't the religion or the principles of the religion, it is the traditions that we have accumulated along the way that create the differential.'*

Loving Ourselves

'What we are longing for and yearning for is what can enable us to rise to much greater heights of strength than we would ever have imagined.' SCILLA ELWORTHY

What about love for ourselves? In the Tibetan Buddhist tradition, the Loving Kindness meditation begins with cultivating a sense of loving kindness and compassion toward *ourselves,* before extending that sentiment toward our loved ones, our enemies, and even the world at large.

The Irish wit and author Oscar Wilde famously wrote: *'To love oneself is the beginning of a lifelong romance.'* Love for oneself gives us inner strength, the foundation upon which all else is built. Jack Canfield tells us what self-love and self-esteem mean to him: *'If you don't love yourself, you're not going to take a stand for yourself. You're not going to stand up against abuse, you're not going to take a stand for your dreams. And you will allow yourself to be abused or used,'* he says.

'Self-esteem is kind of the bottom ground of the field upon which everything else is built. I don't think that you can get to self-actualization without self-esteem, self-acceptance, self- expression, and then you can self-actualize afterwards.'

Scilla Elworthy has this to say on self-love: *'We have to learn to be compassionate and gentle with ourselves before we can do the same in our relationships with other people, and to really listen inside to what our needs are.'* Loving ourselves helps us to change from the inside out. And when we change ourselves, we change the world.

Our Choice Point – You Choose

'Organizations face every day the choice between deep change or slow death. Individuals are facing the choice – deep change or slow death.' ROBERT E. QUINN

We are at a crucial time in history where we face the greatest number of crises ever to face a human population. This is our Choice Point. But these crises can help us become leaders for change, as Robert E. Quinn tells us: *'Crises push us outside our comfort zone. We think, "That was a terrible experience," but if we look at them carefully, there were these amazing things we learned. And now we learn to be leaders.'*

He says that is where we have to go, *'because at that place we become a magnet for energy to fall into the system and for people to have real visions, for people to make real change. If I change myself, I change the world.'*

And there is no better time than the present to change ourselves. Gregg Braden reminds us that Choice Points occur when a cycle comes to an end, in the space in between the end of one cycle and the beginning of a new one. *'It is that place in between the cycles that gives us the opportunity to change the pattern of the previous cycle before we begin the next,'* he says.

And, as we said at the start of this book, we believe the number and scale of the crises facing us indicate that a cycle is coming to an end. The crucial thing now is what choices we will make, for it is our choices at this time that will have the greatest effect on our future.

For Gregg, this belief is encapsulated in the teachings of some indigenous traditions which says that, *'at the end of the day, the Sun disappears from the horizon. It is no longer daylight, but it is not quite night. This is called the crack between the worlds. And the crack between the worlds is when the ancestors say that our prayers have the greatest potency.*

'Another crack between the worlds occurs when the sky becomes light in the morning, but the Sun is yet to rise. It is not really daytime yet, but nor is it nighttime. It is the place in between. They say that is when our prayers are the most potent. Or between every inhale of a breath, and the exhale that follows, there is a place where neither exists. And it is in those places where mystical, magical opportunities occur.'

The choices that we make now – both individually and collectively – are important. And we must not repeat what we have always done. We need to find a better way, and that way is to change ourselves.

Scilla Elworthy sums this up her way: *'Einstein said that we can't solve a problem using the same consciousness that created it. And all my experience over 67 years tells me this is true. We have to somehow shift the perspective that we are coming from.*

'And since our planet is faced with such serious challenges at the moment, challenges of overpopulation, starvation, climate change, pollution, and so on, we can't go on using the same thought patterns that created those problems to try to solve them. So we need to shift. And to my way of thinking, that shift has to happen within the individual.'

We Have the Power

We have to make changes within ourselves and choose the power of love over the love of power. That will inevitably lead to us changing the way we do things, as Scilla says: *'Instead of competing with each other all the time and fighting to earn more money, or fighting to sell more things, or fighting to consume more things, we can take a step back and see what it's like to actually do good things for the common good.'*

And as each person takes this step back, it inspires others to follow as the pattern grows. Scilla talks about the benefits of having a map that would identify people who are trying to make a positive difference in the world, so that they might come together and work together for the common good.

'If Google Earth were to do a map, which I am encouraging them to do, that enabled people to identify themselves as someone who is putting their energies toward a better world in whatever way, people who identify themselves as this kind of change-maker could then appear on Google Earth as a little point of light, and there might be, there probably are, 25 others in their immediate vicinity.

'If you were identified on Google Earth, you would be able to see the others and find them. That would be, I think, the greatest service Google could provide to the world. Google Peace on Earth.' That would be an inspiring map.

Our message to you is this:

We all have the power to change the world, but the change has to take place *inside us*. Every one of us has the capacity to *look within*, discover where we are not aligning with patterns that support a better world, and then *be the change*. We can turn our personal skills toward *doing good*. We can *align* ourselves with higher principles. We all have the capacity to *embrace the power of love.*

We encourage you to understand your world, align your purpose with solutions that help the world, and then to *be* the change you want to see in the world. Jodi Orton tells us, *'I live by a motto that says each and every day we have the chance to make a difference in the life of another person.'*

Seek out the difference you can make. We invite you to have courage and stand up in support of the power of love. Just like the butterfly, we can turn crises into transformation. We can treat each other with kindness and respect. We can build better relationships. As Robert E. Quinn tells us: *'Everybody can make a positive difference.'*

We can choose the power of love or the love of power. That is the Choice Point we face today.

What do you choose?

THE VISIONARIES

Birke Baehr

Twelve-year-old American Birke Baehr is a leading youth advocate for sustainable agriculture and part of a new generation of ecologically aware young people. Birke's passion began at the age of eight, and he has since studied with some of the world's leaders in organic and sustainable agriculture. He plans to be an organic and biodynamic farmer himself one day, but in the meantime, he is writing a kids' book about his journey of discovery about food and farming. He also travels widely, championing environmentally friendly farming practices and safer, more nutritious food.

Tony Benn

Anthony "Tony" Benn emerged as a leading figure in Britain's Labour Party during the 1970s, and later became one of the country's most popular politicians. Tony left parliament in 2001, but remained in the public eye as the first president of the Stop the War Coalition. He continues to fight for his core principles and beliefs in both public and private life, serving as a vocal champion of the underprivileged, disenfranchised, and underrepresented. Tony's passion in the antiwar movement has inspired many, as has his vision for a more just world.

Gregg Braden

Described as a 'rare blend of scientist, visionary, and scholar,' Gregg Braden is the author of numerous internationally bestselling books and DVDs that bridge science and spirituality. Originally a computer geologist and computer systems designer, Gregg ventured outside his field on a personal quest to gather ancient wisdom, esoteric knowledge, and spiritual insight. He has been a pioneer in showing how history, ancient cultures and traditions, and 'lost' knowledge impact and inform today's world and may shape humanity's future. Gregg teaches workshops and conducts seminars and lectures around the world.

Richard Branson

British entrepreneur and adventurer Richard Branson is the founder of the Virgin Group, which today holds more than 200 other companies – an impressive achievement for a man who struggled at school because of learning difficulties caused by dyslexia. In addition to his business acumen, Richard is internationally known for his daring spirit and one-of-a-kind adventures. Unafraid of failure, Richard displays a passion for life that is inspirational. From humble beginnings, he has amassed a self-made fortune and has pushed himself to realize his full potential in both the business and sports worlds.

Peter Buffett

Emmy Award-winning American musician Peter Buffett is the third son of billionaire investor Warren Buffett. Peter has been lauded for his many talents as a performing artist, songwriter, composer, producer, and recording engineer. He is also the author of a bestselling book, *Life Is What You Make It: Finding Your Own Path to Fulfillment*. Beyond music and publishing, Peter is a committed philanthropist and advocate for social change and justice. He is the co-chairman of the NoVo Foundation, which fosters a culture of partnership and collaboration, and which seeks to empower women and girls.

James Caan

Born Nazim Khan, James Caan's family moved from Pakistan to Britain when he was a child. He has risen to become a premier figure in British and Pakistani entrepreneurship and philanthropy, and has founded or cofounded many successful international companies. James has also devoted himself, through private and government organizations, to passing on guidance and training to aspiring business owners and entrepreneurs. He invests in people, helping them to realize their business dreams, and in the coming generations, by funding education and job skills programs, mainly in Pakistan.

Jack Canfield

American Jack Canfield is helping to usher in a new paradigm in the human potential and transformational living. His bestselling *Chicken Soup for the Soul* series of books, coauthored with Mark Victor Hansen, and many audio programs about building high self-esteem and accelerating personal achievement, have helped millions of people to revitalize their lives and realize their dreams. Jack has also taken his message to prisoners, welfare recipients, and inner-city youth. Today he runs his own radio show, has a syndicated newspaper column, and continues to lecture and lead workshops around the world.

John Paul DeJoria

John Paul DeJoria's journey exemplifies the 'rags-to-riches' triumph of the human spirit, teaching us by example what can be accomplished by applying passion and perseverance and believing in yourself. DeJoria's experiences range from hard work at an early age, to homelessness, to single parenthood, and from learning the business ropes to entrepreneurship to founding a wildly successful multinational company. He gives millions of dollars to support charitable causes of all kinds, and as a philanthropist participated in the White House Conference on Philanthropy in Washington, D.C.

Larry Dossey

Texas physician Larry Dossey is a pioneer of mind-body medicine, originally risking his medical reputation to step into the 'new paradigm' of healthcare to support the integration of mind and body, and science and spirituality. His books about spirituality in healing, premonitions, nonlocal mind, and other subjects that bridge science and spirit have reached millions, and consistently make the bestseller lists. His message has reached the hallowed halls of academia, helping to foster the creation of dozens of mind body spirit health programmes in medical schools.

Bill Drayton

Bill Drayton is a social entrepreneur. His passion as a social visionary started as a young boy, seeing the disparity in ways people lived in India, continued as a student at Harvard University and Oxford, and has informed his life and work since. He follows this passion as vigorously as ever, through his global nonprofit foundation Ashoka: Innovators for the Public, and more recently Youth Venture, a project dedicated to encouraging social entrepreneurship in young people. In 2011, Drayton won Spain's prestigious Prince of Asturias Awards for International Cooperation for his work promoting entrepreneurs.

Scilla Elworthy

Scotland's Scilla Elworthy founded the Oxford Research Group, an independent, nongovernmental organization that facilitates dialogue between the world's nuclear powers and their critics, work for which she was awarded the Niwano Peace Prize and was nominated for the Nobel Peace Prize three times. Scilla left that organization in 2002 to found Peace Direct, a charity that funds and supports grassroots peace-related initiatives in conflict-ridden parts of the world. Scilla is a member of the World Future Council, and has been instrumental in the development or creation of many cultural and political endeavors.

Barbara Marx Hubbard

Transformational living, ecological awareness, peace and resolution, personal development, and self-realization – these are all areas in which American Barbara Marx Hubbard has fostered positive change and continues to leave her mark. She is the cofounder and chairperson of the Foundation for Conscious Evolution, and works with The Shift Network as a guide and teacher for conscious evolution. A speaker and social innovator, and the author of six books, Barbara has been a tireless champion of the Earth's future since the 1960s, and is a unique voice for communicating the message of conscious evolution for humanity.

Brett Moran

Britain's Brett Moran is a motivational speaker and transformation guru who combines energy, work, and the power of the mind to help others to heal. Brett specializes in addiction recovery – particularly from heroin, crack, alcohol, and other severely addicting substances. A former addict himself, Brett combines many complementary therapies to help his clients transform the belief patterns and perceptions that foster their addictive behavior. Brett has also worked with prisoners, the homeless, at-risk youth, and others who often do not have access to the newest therapeutic approaches.

Jodi Orton

Jodi Orton was a successful career woman when she and her husband, Brett, made the life-choice to become foster parents. Over the past 20 years they have provided a loving home to more than 100 foster children, as well as adopting nine children – soon to be 10! They nurture their ever-growing family on a wildlife rescue reserve in the American Midwest surrounded by nature and animals. Many of their foster children have special needs and require constant attention; the Ortons also offer emergency short-term foster care for children at especially high risk.

Alison Pothier

British inspirational speaker, intuitive healer, and coach Alison Pothier enjoyed a successful career as a chief operating officer and managing director of an international investment bank before founding Inside Out Retreats, an organization through which she offers programs, treatments, and events that foster personal transformation. Alison combines her business and transpersonal skills to promote insight, consciousness-raising, and transformation. From public workshops to corporate consulting, her reach extends far and wide, fostering new paradigm thinking to make a positive impact in both the private and professional worlds.

Robert E. Quinn

American Robert E. Quinn is at the forefront of change, especially in the business world. He is a professor of business and management at the University of Michigan's Ross School of Business; a leading speaker on the international circuit; and a consultant to businesses, governments, and volunteer organizations on leadership and organizational change. Robert has written numerous books about positive change, visionary leadership, and social issues in the business arena. He is also a founding partner of Wholonics Leadership Group, which provides guidance for individuals and organizations to realize their goals.

Ian Stewart

Ian Stewart is a professor of mathematics at Britain's University of Warwick. A member of the Royal Society, in 1995 he was awarded the Michael Faraday Medal for achievement in his field. Ian has also received other awards for his work in promoting mathematics and has written many bestselling books, including mathematics textbooks, science fiction, and popular science titles. Among his best-known books are *Fearful Symmetry* and *Does God Play Dice: The New Mathematics of Chaos*.

Archbishop Desmond Tutu

Activist Archbishop Tutu's voice became known to the world in the 1980s through his tireless work to end apartheid in his native South Africa. During that turbulent period, he practiced passive resistance and motivated others through his eloquence, and his adherence to the belief that all people deserve the right to dignity and the pursuit of happiness. He has since taken to the world stage to preach reconciliation, non-violence, and forgiveness and has campaigned to fight AIDS, poverty, and racism. Tutu has received many awards and honors, including the Nobel Peace Prize.

Vlatko Vedral

Serbian-born Vlatko Vedral is a professor of quantum information theory at the University of Oxford in the UK, and is also affiliated with the National University of Singapore's Centre for Quantum Technologies. His book *Decoding Reality: The Universe as Quantum Information* examines in layman's terms how information, rather than energy, is the foundational aspect of the cosmos. Vlatko's revolutionary ideas have furthered our understanding of entropy, determinism, time, quantum mechanics, and other fundamental aspects of reality. His particular areas of research are quantum entanglement and information theory.

Rainer Viehweger

Germany's Dr. Rainer Viehweger trained as a physician in Hungary. For most of his early medical career he worked as an orthopedic surgeon, but later shifted his focus to holistic medicine and, in 2003, opened a private practice devoted to integrating conventional medicine with alternative and complementary medicine. Now trained in many therapies, including acupuncture, Hunecke's neural therapy, trigger shockwave therapy, psychosomatic energetics, and Scenar therapy, Rainer has published articles on both conventional and complementary medicine and a book that explores the physics of global scaling in relation to human biology.

THE CHOICE POINT
ALIGN YOUR PURPOSE
TRANSFORMATION PROGRAM

Align Your Purpose is a groundbreaking new Transformation Program designed to complement this book. It takes the Choice Point philosophy and shows you how to lead the life you were born to live – one filled with purpose, achievement, contentment, and contribution.

Created by Choice Point's authors, Harry Massey and David Hamilton, and in special collaboration with Emotional Freedom Techniques (EFT) healer and author Sasha Allenby, Align Your Purpose will enable you to:

- Understand how the universe exchanges information and energy with everything that exists within it... including you.

- Tune in to the information and energy that is already unfolding and shaping your world, so you can clearly see the best path to your future.

- Gain insightful wisdom that will instill in you the knowledge that in taking this path, your life will head in the direction that best serves you... and the world.

- Explore and test your passions and skill sets to reveal your undeniable purpose in life with crystal-clear vision.

- Align your purpose with the evolving patterns in your world to harness the power of the universe, and have it working for your better future as opposed to against it.

- Cultivate an abundance of self-courage and make the necessary changes to capitalize on your personal and global transformation potential.

Designed with everyone in mind – from absolute beginners to seasoned experts – and with simple and practical exercises to follow, you will be able to create a clear understanding of your world and a solid foundation for transforming your life for the better.

All of the principles outlined in this book are broken down into easy-to-follow steps that you can apply to your life to create changes. This important, interactive, multimedia Transformation Program will enable you to learn from global leaders in transformation – including Sir Richard Branson, Archbishop Desmond Tutu, John Paul DeJoria, Barbara Marx Hubbard, Gregg Braden, Jack Canfield, Arielle Ford, Peter Buffett, Scilla Elworthy, and many more.

Supported by never-before-seen interviews with these transformational leaders from the Choice Point movie, and a brand new commentary by Harry Massey and David Hamilton, you will not only be inspired to undergo your own personal transformation, but encouraged to leave your mark by creating a transformation on a larger, global scale too.

You will also be invited to participate in the Choice Point movement, where you can share your transformational journey with other like-minded people in our global community, and lend your voice to our common cause... a better future for you and a better world for all.

Join us. Transform your life. And help make the world a better place for our future generations.

For more details, or to sign up for the Transformation Program, please visit, www.alignyourpurpose.com.

REFERENCES

Preface

1.   Gregg Braden, *Fractal Time*, Hay House, 2009

Chapter 1: The Common Thread

1.   E. Friedman, 'Menstrual and lunar cycles,' *American Journal of Obstetrics and Gynecology*, 1981, 140(3), 350

2.   S. P. Law, 'The regulation of menstrual cycle and its relationship to the Moon,' *Acta. Obstetricia et Gynecologica Scandinavica*, 1986, 65, 45-48

3.   S. M. Hsiang, K. C. Meng, and M. A. Cane, 'Civil Conflicts are associated with the global climate,' *Nature*, 2011, 476, 428–441

4.   A. Krivilyova and C. Robotti, 'Playing the field: Geomagnetic storms and the stock market,' *Federal Reserve Bank of Atlanta, working paper*, 2003–5b, October 2003

Chapter 2: Understanding and Predicting Patterns

1.   David R. Hamilton, *Why Kindness is Good for You*, Hay House, London, 2009

Chapter 6: Does My Purpose Make a Difference?

1.   A. Szeto, D. A. Nation, A. J. Mendez, J. Dominguez-Bendela, L. G. Brooks, N. Schneiderman, and P. M. McCabe, 'Oxytocin attenuates NADP-dependent superoxide activity and IL-6 secretion in macrophages and vascular cells,' *American Journal of Endocrinology and Metabolism*, 2008, 295, E1, 495-501

2.   David R. Hamilton, *Why Kindness is Good for You*, Hay House, 2009

3.   'Social relationships and mortality risk: a meta-analytic review,' *PLoS Medicine*, 2010, 7(7), e1,000, 316, 1–20

Chapter 7: How to Be the Change

1.   David R. Hamilton, *The Contagious Power of Thinking*, Hay House, 2011 and references cited within

ACKNOWLEDGMENTS

Harry Massey

I would first like to thank my family, especially my mum and my brother, for their constant support over the years and for believing in me – and my partner, David, for his continual love and patience with everything I do.

I'm also grateful to the professional and inspirational team at Halo Films, especially Peter Georgi and Myfanwy Marshall for putting some real structure into the *Choice Point* movie and bringing out the best in everyone in the interviews. Not forgetting all the camera and sound crews who supported us throughout the filming.

I also appreciate the work of Melanie Provan, for helping in the early stages to get the *Choice Point* project off the ground.

Heartfelt thanks also to Jitu Patel for your trust and believing in the vision of *Choice Point* and to the key *Choice Point* team, including Prash Patel, Charlie Stuart-Gay, Trina Hart, and Andrea Evans. Your continued commitment and passion for *Choice Point* has helped make my vision a reality and is helping to change the world.

My appreciation also goes to all the team at NES Health, especially Peter Fraser, Marcel Vischers, and Dave Court, who have supported me in following my vision over the last 10 years and have enabled me to move on to new projects by ensuring everything at NES is well-managed.

And I am grateful to my co-author, David Hamilton, for all his time and hard work and for bringing this book to life in a way that everyone can understand. You have been a delight to work with. Also huge thanks to Sasha Allenby, who spent months in the early phases teasing concepts out of me and onto paper, so that the film, the book, and the course could be made.

Thank you, also, to the 'Brockway Boys' for supporting *Choice Point* in your many different ways.

And finally, a great big thank-you to all the change-makers, for giving your time, thoughts, and energy into sharing your beliefs and experience. Without you, none of this would have been possible. I am truly grateful.

David Hamilton

I'd first like to express my gratitude to my partner, Elizabeth Caproni. Her constant support has been the common thread through my development as an author. I am deeply grateful for her love and her patience, especially when I spent so many hours at my desk instead of in her company.

Warmest thanks to all the staff at Hay House, and in particular Michelle Pilley, Jo Lal, and Jo Burgess, who have individually played a significant part in my life over the past 5 years. Thanks also to Lizzie Hutchins for editorial advice in the early stages of writing this book. And I would also like to say thank you to Julie Oughton, who was always so accommodating in amending timelines when new interviews meant that new material had to be added to the book.

I am especially grateful for our editor, Debra Wolter, who helped to shape the book and greatly simplify some of the technical material by asking just the right questions.

And finally, I would like to express my gratitude to Harry Massey, who has inspired me with his insight and intelligence, and helped me to see many more possibilities in how I can positively contribute to the world. I am grateful that he gave me the opportunity to work on this book with him, and to make a difference in the world in this way.

The staff at Caffè Nero in Windsor also deserve some thanks for creating a warm, friendly atmosphere that was just what I needed to write.

JOIN THE HAY HOUSE FAMILY

As the leading self-help, mind, body and spirit publisher in the UK, we'd like to welcome you to our family so that you can enjoy all the benefits our website has to offer.

 EXTRACTS from a selection of your favourite author titles

 COMPETITIONS, PRIZES & SPECIAL OFFERS Win extracts, money off, downloads and so much more

 LISTEN to a range of radio interviews and our latest audio publications

 CELEBRATE YOUR BIRTHDAY An inspiring gift will be sent your way

 **LATEST NEWS** Keep up with the latest news from and about our authors

 ATTEND OUR AUTHOR EVENTS Be the first to hear about our author events

 iPHONE APPS Download your favourite app for your iPhone

 HAY HOUSE INFORMATION Ask us anything, all enquiries answered

join us online at **www.hayhouse.co.uk**

 292B Kensal Road, London W10 5BE
T: 020 8962 1230 E: info@hayhouse.co.uk

ABOUT THE AUTHORS

Harry Massey is a writer, director, entrepreneur, and visionary. He directed the full-length documentary film *Choice Point* and co-wrote this accompanying book. Harry founded Choice Point to bring his vision for transforming the world to the general public. Its mission is both to inspire people to transform themselves – and so to be the change they want to see in the world – and to develop paradigm-changing technology that can assist us in solving some of the world's most pressing problems. In addition, Massey co-founded NES Health Limited (www.neshealth.com), a company dedicated to furthering a 21st-century system of natural holistic health care based on integrating physics and biology. Massey was also executive producer and co-writer of the 2009 best-selling documentary DVD *The Living Matrix: A New Science of Healing*, which championed the rise of a new kind of medicine based on energy and information fields.

After completing his Ph.D., **David Hamilton** worked for four years in the pharmaceutical industry developing drugs for cardiovascular disease and cancer. During this time he also served as an athletics coach and the manager of one of the UK's largest athletics clubs, which he lead to three successive UK finals. Upon leaving the pharmaceutical industry, David co-founded the international relief charity Spirit Aid Foundation and served as a director for two years. While writing his first book, David taught chemistry and ecology at James Watt College of Further and Higher Education and tutored chemistry at Glasgow University. Now a best-selling author of 6 books published by Hay House, he offers talks and workshops that use science to inspire. David writes a regular blog for the *Huffington Post*. www.drdavidhamilton.com.